SPEED READING
WITH THE
RIGHT BRAIN

Praise for
SPEED READING WITH THE RIGHT BRAIN

Unlike many other "speed reading" strategies available, Speed *Reading with the Right Brain* is not a gimmick; it's a unique method that allows you to more effectively assimilate what you read in a shorter amount of time.

Amanda Johnson, M.A.,
Assistant Professor of English, Collin College, Plano, Texas

David Butler and I have been friends for five years and have enjoyed many interesting conversations about reading and comprehension. I have always found his thoughts on this subject to be incredibly unique and insightful. Speed Reading with the Right Brain has given David a place to collect these ideas in one place, and make them easy to understand for anyone wishing to improve their reading skills.

This book includes not only original theories and techniques for reading improvement, but also a totally exclusive method of presenting practice exercises that makes it extremely easy to begin reading whole ideas at a time.

Pick up this book and start reading with your whole brain.

Richard Sutz, CEO,
The Literacy Company, www.EfficientReading.com,
Author of "Speed Reading for Dummies"

I strongly recommend David Butler's new book Speed *Reading with the Right Brain* as one of the most innovate new approaches to speed reading on the market today. For the past year, Dave and I have discussed in email exchanges crucial issues about reading comprehension and the history of speed reading instructions. Dave's unique approach emphasizes the importance of reading with the right side of the brain which helps the reader quickly comprehend a text by converting groups of words into images and concepts.

It is amazing to me that so much could have been written in so many years since Evelyn Wood about speed reading and no one came up with the idea of "speed comprehension." All the other programs emphasize rapid eye movement over text, promising that comprehension would follow, which it usually didn't. The concept of focusing on comprehension first has been the missing link.

Speed Reading with the Right Brain, is a "must read" for peoples interested in improving their reading comprehension and speed.

Dr. James Young,
Professor of English, Weber State University, Ogden, Utah

In the last few thousand years, reading has gone from a mystical ability of the few, to a way of experiencing the world beyond people's local existence, to a method of self-improvement. But with today's accelerating pace of information, reading has truly become an essential *survival skill*.

Speed Reading with the Right Brain demonstrates how to improve your reading by *thinking conceptually*, which means thinking about what things really are rather than just their name. This is a powerful method for improving this most important factor in education and success.

All skills require practice, but some practice is more effective than others. This very unique method of displaying text makes learning to read faster so much easier.

Austin Butler,
President and Founder, Teaching.com

David Butler gets to the core of reading comprehension in *Speed Reading with the Right Brain*, with effective techniques and exercises to focus your attention on meaning versus words. This book will speed up your reading, increase your comprehension, and make reading a pleasurable pursuit of new worlds of knowledge rather than slow torture that only leads to confusion. Read it and learn!

Danielle Ellis,
Mother, editor, and 6th grade teacher

Table of Contents

Introduction

I slammed the book shut. Why was I such a frustratingly slow reader? And why couldn't I remember what I read?

I was sitting in my yard, in the shade of the tall white birch trees, beneath the blue summer sky, reading a book I was very interested in. But I couldn't help getting angry at how much time the reading was taking me and how poor my comprehension was. How could I enjoy a book if I had to read it in slow motion? And then just forget it all?

This was me several years ago. And if this sounds like you, read on. I can show you how to read faster and understand more, by reading with more of your brain; specifically, the powerful, intuitive, big-picture right hemisphere. Although not normally associated with reading, this side of your head has a unique capability of quickly visualizing and conceptualizing entire complex ideas.

Reading with the right brain is a technique which opened the doors to reading for me. This is not like any other technique you may have already tried; believe me, I've tried them all. This is different.

This book is about learning to read conceptually and imagining and visualizing what you are reading. Reading conceptually is not just another speed reading trick, but a different way of thinking. By learning to use your right brain's visualizing abilities, you can end the lazy habit of merely reciting words, and learn to really think about the ideas.

Visualizing is central to this technique and therefore will be mentioned repeatedly in different contexts throughout the book. But this book also explains how stronger comprehension leads to faster reading, how the history of reading developed, and how the brain manages to accomplish this miracle. Plus, there's a discussion of how to side-step bad reading habits and an examination of popular speed reading myths.

The jewel of this book though is the set of 20 unique reading exercises, which make it easy to learn to read with the right brain by guiding your attention to each of the short, meaningful pieces of information which sentences are made of. These specially formatted exercises will give you an easy way to experience how it feels to read faster and to read with better comprehension. By spending a little time practicing with these exercises, you can discover the power of reading with the right brain.

Frustration

I had always wished I was a better reader. I wanted to read more but I was so slow. I was interested in non-fiction books, especially history and science, but if the point of reading non-fiction was to acquire and retain knowledge, then this was probably the single least effective activity I ever engaged in. Not only was I slow, but after spending dozens of hours getting to the end of a book, I only retained the foggiest idea of what I had read.

I had always been frustrated by how much time my reading took. And no matter how much I read, I was still slow. I wanted to improve but didn't know how. Nothing I tried worked.

As a young boy, I would see advertisements that promised to teach me to "speed read." I don't remember what these courses cost, but it must have been more than I could afford on my allowance.

In high school, I finally had the chance to take a night course on speed reading—one night a week for ten weeks. An impressive looking machine displayed text in short segments, one at a time, with a control for speed adjustment. It seemed like this should work for sure, but in the end, it had no real effect. The faster the text displayed, the worse my comprehension was.

I tried several speed reading books and courses during high school, college, and beyond, but was always disappointed.

Reading well should have been in my genes. My father and mother were excellent readers. My mother loved to read fiction and my father loved non-fiction. My father was self-taught since 8th grade, but because of his passion for reading, he could speak intelligently on practically any subject.

But it didn't look like I had inherited my parents' reading skills. I also found it difficult to maintain concentration and I had a horrible memory. What was wrong with me? Maybe I just had a slow brain. Maybe I could never read faster.

Discovery

Then one day at the age of 49, in the summer of 2000, I was sitting in my yard trying to get through a book on the interesting science of fractals. But again, it was a struggle.

I couldn't stand it anymore. It seemed stupid to spend so much time reading with so little to show for it. I shut the book.

I sat holding the closed book, wondering if I should force myself to continue reading. I didn't know what to do. I would be a quitter if I gave up, but a fool to waste so much time on a beautiful summer day.

I reopened the book and stared at the page... and then something interesting happened. As my mind idled, I began to notice patterns in the arrangement of the words. The rows of spaces seemed to form horizontal, slanted, and vertical lines that outlined blocks of words.

The discovery of such behavior is one of the important achievements of chaos theory. Another is the methodologies which have been designed for a precise scientific evaluation of the presence of chaotic behavior in mathematical models as well as in real phenomena. Using these methodologies, it is now possible, in principle, to estimate the 'predictability horizon' of a system. This is the mathematical, physical, or time parameter limit within which predictability is ideally possible and beyond which we will never be able to predict with certainty. It has been established, for example, that the predictability horizon in weather forecasting is not more than about two or three weeks. This means that no matter how many more weather stations are included in the observation, no matter how much more accurately weather data are collected and analyzed, we will never be able to predict the weather with any degree of numerical accuracy beyond this horizon of time.

But before we go into an introductory discussion of what chaos theory is trying to accomplish, let us look at some historical aspects of the field. If we look at the development of the sciences on a time-scale on which the efforts of our forbears are visible, we will observe indications of an apparent recapitulation in the present day, even if at a different level. To people during

I played with this illusion for a while, but then this mental rest stop led me to wonder if there were patterns in the ideas too. Just as these clumps of words formed *visual* patterns, there were probably clumps of words that created patterns of *ideas*. What if reading in "idea clumps" would make reading faster?

Grouping letters into words is easy because of the spaces between words, but what about ideas? Ideas usually require multiple words; shorter than sentences, but long enough to form complete pieces of understandable information. What if I tried to concentrate on these complete ideas instead of individual words? I grabbed a pencil from the house and started marking off groups of what I thought sounded like meaningful chunks of words with slashes like this:

But before / we go into / an introductory discussion / of what chaos theory / is trying to accomplish, / let us look / at some historical aspects / of the field. / If we look / at the development / of the sciences / on a time-scale / on which / the efforts / of our forebears / are visible, / we will observe / indications / of an apparent / recapitulation / in the present day, / even if / at a different level.

And wow! Suddenly when I read these phrases as complete units of meaning, the ideas seemed to jump off the page, straight into my mind!

I marked up and read several more pages. This looked like a breakthrough. I could read the text faster, plus the text was easier to understand.

This was the solution I had been looking for. There was one problem though. How could I read like this without needing to first manually mark up the text?

As a design engineer, it was difficult to leave a problem like this alone. In fact, it was more like the idea owned *me* than vice versa. It was an interesting challenge, and it also looked like it might help me overcome my long-time struggle with reading.

A few weeks later, I came up with an interesting idea for a computer program that could automatically divide text into meaningful phrases. After learning a little programming, I put together a test of this idea and tried this automatic phrase-parser on some text from an online news story. I displayed the phrases one at a time and I was immediately convinced that I was on to something. The results weren't perfect, but it definitely made the text faster to read and easier to understand.

Development

After this discovery, I spent the next few years improving the algorithm, and also making the program available online (see bonus section at end of book), to see if others had the same response I did. This original online reading tool resulted in plenty of positive feedback, which in turn, motivated me even more to continue working on it.

I was sleeping late one morning in January 2009, when I was woken by a phone call. It was the CEO of a company that teaches speed reading. He had seen my website and wanted to discuss licensing my algorithm for use in his own software. This very nice gentleman flew out to California for a couple of meetings, and over the next few months we worked out an agreement and signed a licensing contract.

I was walking on a cloud. Imagine, licensing my idea! But unfortunately the deteriorating economy had other plans for me. After several more meetings with the CEO and working for months with his company programmer to add this new feature to their software, business slowed and things ground to a halt. Their updated software was never released, and eventually it became evident that it probably never would be.

But while working with this company, something else happened. They had asked me to help them develop lesson plans around this method, and the plans I came up with are what led to several discoveries and a new online course (see bonus section at end of book).

The company had also asked for my ideas about why this method worked so well. It was in coming up with answers to these questions that I realized faster reading mostly required faster thinking, and the only effective way to think faster is to process more information at a time— that is, to read whole ideas or phrases, instead of words.

I could see that reading these phrases was a faster way to read and comprehend, but reading this way also took more concentration, and this level of concentration was sometimes difficult to maintain. What could a reader do to hold their attention on the larger ideas?

Then I discovered that if I *visualized* what I was reading, I would automatically think in larger concepts. By concentrating on visual images, I was encouraging my brain to think of the larger ideas. Even if I couldn't always think of an actual image, the attempt to visualize was still focusing my attention on mental concepts rather than words.

As I thought about this visualizing technique, I realized I'd seen something like this before. *Drawing on the Right Side of the Brain* by Betty Edwards is a very effective book for learning to draw. The book was first published in 1979, when the science of lateral brain function was new. The book explained how, contrary to how the left brain merely described things, the right brain thought in pictures; and by suppressing the descriptions on the left side, you could use the special right brain talent to actually draw what you saw instead of what you thought you saw.

This seemed similar to what I was doing when visualizing the phrases. I was using my visual right hemisphere to imagine the real concepts of what I was reading.

We don't need to explore any of this science in detail, but only need to understand that each side of the brain works in a very different way. For those with a computer background, basically the left brain works as a serial processor, and the right brain works as a parallel processor. This means the left brain handles information one step at a time, while the right brain looks at whole patterns of information simultaneously.

The result is that the two sides have different personalities and see the world in very different ways. But it's the partnership of this odd couple that lets us make careful analyses as well as leaps of intuition.

Recognizing this, it became apparent where my difficulty in reading had occurred. I was concentrating heavily on the left-brain function of decoding words, and was leaving the real comprehension of ideas pretty much to chance. But this was all I was ever taught in school. Word-recognition is where most reading instruction ends.

Most of the more advanced reading improvement courses also only concentrate on the left brain function of recognizing words, but then just having you try to recognize them faster.

Tapping the right brain was the answer, and understanding how to do this could be a big help. Even though the online course was very effective and well-received, I saw there was still a need for a clearer explanation of how and why this worked, and how to best apply this method. Collecting, clarifying, and organizing these ideas is what led to this book.

This approach to improving reading skills is different from previous approaches because it doesn't suggest pushing your speed and waiting for your comprehension to catch up. Instead, it teaches you how to strengthen your comprehension and then let your reading speed increase on its own. This is not a subtle difference. To read faster you must forget about how *fast* you are reading and put all your attention on *what* you are reading.

If you have any questions while using this book, please contact me at the address or website listed at the end of the book.

But first I want to tell you a joke.

Initial Speed Test

On the following page, there is a quick test to determine your current reading speed. This short test will only take about a minute to read.

The test is in the form of a joke. A joke is used to guarantee comprehension, because who likes to read a joke without getting it? This means you won't need to take a "comprehension" test because, as with any joke, you'll know if you "get it" or not.

For this test, read *exactly* the way you would *normally* read. Don't worry about getting a low score, and don't try to read faster than your normal speed. This will be your "before" picture.

Use a stopwatch (there are several free ones available on the internet) or use a clock and subtract your starting time from your ending time to find how long it takes you to read the test. You can download a form for recording your initial speed and your later exercise results at bit.ly/2bfdGpV.

After starting your stopwatch or making a note of your start time, immediately begin reading the text on the next page. When you have finished reading, make a note of your reading time and calculate your words per minute.

When you're ready, start the clock, turn to the next page, and begin. Remember, read at your normal speed.

A wife was preparing a breakfast of fried eggs for her husband when he suddenly burst into the kitchen.

"Careful!" he said. "Careful! Put in some more butter! Oh, my gosh! You're cooking too many at once!

"Too many! Turn them! Turn them now! Now! We need more butter! Oh, my gosh! They're going to stick!

"Slow things down a bit! Careful! Careful! I said be careful! You never listen to me when you're cooking! Never!

"Right, turn them! Hurry up! Turn them now! Are you crazy? Have you lost your mind? Don't forget to salt them. You know you always forget to salt them. Use the salt. USE THE SALT! USE THE SALT! USE THE SALT!"

The wife stared at him in disbelief. "What the heck is wrong with you? Do you think I don't know how to fry a couple of eggs?

The husband replied calmly, "I just wanted to show you what it feels like when I'm driving."

Stop Your Timer Now

Note the length of time in seconds
(e.g. 1 minute 15 seconds = 75 seconds).

Next, calculate your reading speed in words per minute (WPM) by dividing the number of words (which is 152) by the seconds you took to read, and then multiplying by sixty.

WPM Formula:

$$words / seconds \times 60 = WPM$$

For example, if the reading time was seventy-five seconds, your calculation would be:

$$152 \text{ words} / 75 \text{ seconds} \times 60 = 122 \text{ WPM}$$

When you have completed your calculation, record your speed for later reference.

Note that although there were 161 *actual* words, we will use the common standard length of 5.5 characters per word—that's 4.5 average characters per word plus one space between each word. This will give more consistent results regardless of changing word lengths among exercises.

What Your Speed Means

Based on studies of average adult readers, here are some basic speed categories:

- 1 out of 2 adults can read 200 WPM ("average" readers)
- 1 out of 10 adults can read 300 WPM ("good" readers)
- 1 out of 100 adults can read 400 WPM ("fast" readers)
- 1 out of 1,000 adults can read 600 WPM ("speed" readers)

This should give you a general idea of the distribution of speeds. Notice that only one out of every one hundred adults, reads faster than four hundred words per minute. This is interesting because this seems to be a common plateau for many people. It is like some sort of physical speed limit.

Exceeding four hundred words per minute appears to require a fundamental shift in mindset; readers can only pass this speed when they stop thinking of the words.

Actual speed readers (over 600 WPM) are a particularly rarified group. In fact, it makes me wonder where all the graduates of the many speed reading courses are—those courses that claim you can easily learn to read thousands of words per minute—because these people certainly are not showing up in any of the statistics.

But these statistics are not meant to discourage you, only to offer a reality check. Even reading four hundred words per minute is an excellent skill to have and a very achievable one with this method. If a two-hundred-words-per-minute reader could double his or her speed to four hundred words per minute, this would be an excellent result which would definitely be worth their effort.

This does not mean it's not possible to continue improving to six hundred words per minute and beyond, but you can never know how far any individual can go since reading aptitudes are as unique as basketball or bowling aptitudes. But with proper understanding of the processes and techniques in this book, you will be on the path to reaching your maximum potential.

Chapter 1: Getting Started

Thank you for purchasing this book and for your *time*. Time has become a rare commodity, and I truly appreciate you giving me the opportunity to share an idea that has changed my life. It has been an adventure to write this book and to develop the supporting concepts and theories. I am honored to be allowed to share this with you.

Background

The theory of reading conceptually came to me after years of personal frustration. I am sixty-three years old and had been frustrated with my reading since about the age of ten. By the time I was forty-nine, I was convinced my slow reading was incurable. The idea I had in the summer of 2000, in retrospect, now seems blindingly obvious: READING IS COMPREHENSION.

This idea is more powerful than it might sound. It is this discovery that allowed me to increase my reading speed from 150 words per minute, to a very enjoyable 450-500 words per minute.

The idea stemmed from the realization that comprehension wasn't just a *part* of reading; on the contrary, reading was nothing *but* comprehension. Seeing text and recognizing words, was only the *delivery* process—but it wasn't *reading*. The words delivered raw data to my brain, but this data wasn't actually *read* until I *understood* it.

All those speed reading books, programs, and courses that I'd tried in the past only focused on eye movement and word recognition—that is, learning to *see* words faster. But seeing is not reading.

Many courses even suggested I could completely *ignore* comprehension and somehow good comprehension would come to me AFTER I became a fast reader. But this is never what happened. The faster I pushed my reading, the faster the information seemed to leak out of my brain.

So, why were they telling me that faster reading would result in faster comprehension? It appears that this hypothesis was based on nothing more than the observation that fast readers had good comprehension.

But why assume that fast reading *leads* to good comprehension? Doesn't it make more sense the other way around—that better comprehension leads to faster reading?

After all, what *is* reading? Is it only recognizing and pronouncing words? Obviously not, because there are plenty of words I can recognize and pronounce but still have no idea what they mean.

For example, I can "read" this medical text: "*Aspergillus was detected histopathologically in the visceral pleural cavity.*" But when I say I can read this, I mean I can *say* the words. My mouth and eyes might read this text, but, since I am not a doctor, all my mind processes is "*blah blah blah.*"

Real reading is something that occurs AFTER you recognize the words. It's what happens when you realize what the writer is *saying*, or more exactly what the author was *thinking* when he or she wrote the words.

You haven't read *anything* until you've *comprehended* it.

This is such an important point, that you will find it repeated throughout the book. I apologize if I seem repetitive, but in each case I will actually be discussing this point in a separate context.

Another reason for repeating this point, is that I have discovered it often takes multiple contacts with new ideas before they make firm connections in our minds.

OK, as interesting as all this might be (to me anyway), here's the good part. The exercises in this book are pretty easy to do. Just practice with the specially formatted texts and you will begin reading whole phrases at a time, and go from hearing words to *seeing ideas*.

Why Read Faster?

If you tell someone you are learning to read faster, you will usually hear, *"Why would you want to read faster? How could you enjoy a book if you read it fast? To enjoy your reading, don't you need to read slow enough to listen to the sound of the words, the cadence and rhythm of the language? Wouldn't reading fast destroy the beauty of the story?"*

But think about this. How do you know what speed is best? Unless you're reading aloud, how do you know what the "correct" speed is? Some people read faster and some people read slower. Is *yours*, or *theirs*, the "right" speed?

There is no clock in your mind. Reading speed is very flexible and relative to your thinking speed. If you can comprehend faster, you will be thinking faster, but what you read will always seem to be taking place at "normal" speed in your mind.

But while you may think you are slowly savoring a book, you actually may be missing much of the big picture by reading too slowly to tie the story points together. By the time you get to the middle of the chapter or book, much of the detail and nuance of the beginning may have faded.

The truth is, there is no right speed. If you know how to read faster, you can read faster or slower if you wish. If you have the right tools, you are free to choose the one you prefer for each situation.

Why This Method?

I realize the field of reading improvement has more than its share of carnival sideshows and tacky self-help books—many of them loaded with hype, hucksterism, pop psychology, and pseudoscientific clichés. Plus, most of these books and courses are simply copies of one another. I'm sure you've already noticed this, and I realize any self-appointed guru is likely going to set off your BS detector. So allow me to share some of the comments that were emailed or left on my website about this method:

- *"I have used several speed reading programs, but they were missing what this teaches. This is so terrific. Thanks so much."*
- *"I found your course excellent and more than helpful in improving my reading speed and comprehension."*
- *"... a most enjoyable course that has invigorated my love for reading and learning."*
- *"I was not even an average reader. But now with practice, I'm an average reader working towards being an excellent reader. Thank you."*
- *"Your course is perfect, really! This method makes it more pleasurable to read! Thank you so much!"*
- *"Thanks so much for creating this wonderful tool. I struggle with dyslexia and have become increasingly frustrated with my slow reading speed. I just found your tool today, and I've already raised my reading speed significantly :) Thanks again for creating this wonderful program."*
- *"This is really great for kids to use to increase their reading fluency. It teaches them to read in meaning units or phrases read. It is transferring to their other reading."*
- *"I am seventy-five and only with your course am I able to read in groups of words."*
- *"Great, amazing new tool. Thank you for inventing this. I absolutely love this."*
- *"I use it to help me get through my school work faster and to also read the classics. Thank you!"*
- *"I have been through countless speed reading books, programs, etc. This is by far the best program I have found. Thank you."*
- *"Hello. Thank you so much for this amazing program. I have noticed a great difference in my ability to concentrate, read, and comprehend. Again, thank you so much."*
- *"I really appreciate you making this tool available for all us. I have already doubled my reading speed. Thank you very much."*

I enjoy receiving comments like these. It has been terrific to be able to improve my own reading, but it's been fantastic to hear from other people who have also enjoyed and profited from these ideas.

Layout of This Book

Each chapter of this book starts with instructional material. These explanations will give you an understanding of what reading with the right brain is and how it can be applied to your reading.

The instructional material also includes information about the history of and the mental processes involved in reading. This overview of reading will help you stay on the straightest path to faster reading and better comprehension.

At the end of each chapter there is an exercise to practice what you have learned. Each exercise consists of the first thousand words of a separate popular classic novel.

The text in these exercises is specially formatted in a way that makes it easy to see the phrases. This is done by indicating the separate units of meaning with alternating black and gray text. This will identify the phrases for you, so you can concentrate more on seeing the meaning of each phrase.

Here is an example of this technique.

Alice was beginning to get very tired of sitting by her sister on the bank, and of having nothing to do: once or twice she had peeped into the book her sister was reading, but it had no pictures or conversations in it, 'and what is the use of a book,' thought Alice 'without pictures or conversation?'

In this example, "*Alice was beginning*" is the first unit of meaning, "*to get very tired*" is the second, "*of sitting by her sister*" is the third, etc.

The alternating black and gray text helps you quickly focus your eyes on each phrase, making these phrases easier to grasp at a glance.

Each exercise is one thousand words long. The first eight hundred words are highlighted in black and gray, and the last two hundred words are displayed normally. So after reading phrases with the help of the highlighting, the last two hundred words give you practice picking out phrases on your own. In effect, the first eight hundred highlighted words will give you a bit of a running start at the remaining unformatted text.

Practice these exercises and concentrate on reading whole ideas. Reading text in larger chunks this way will transfer greater amounts of information per glance, like a high-speed broadband form of reading. It will also make reading easier and faster because you will be concentrating on the larger, more meaningful concepts. Reading these larger ideas will put more emphasis on what has always been the true bottleneck of reading speed: *comprehension*.

Comprehension must come first. Instead of pushing your speed while simply trying to retain your comprehension, faster reading will come as the *natural result* of better comprehension. Rather than focusing on *speed reading*, you will be focusing on *speed comprehension*.

In addition to the practice exercises in this book, you can also use the online phrase-reading tool (see online resources section), to practice reading any text in phrases. This book originated from the desire to give a more in-depth explanation of the techniques and theories of phrase-reading. Reading phrases can increase speed and comprehension, but these improvements come easier with a proper understanding of how of this method. Another reason for this book was to supply a more natural reading experience to make phrase-reading practice more comfortable and realistic.

Of course, as with any skill, it will take practice to embed it into your subconscious and really make it your own, but as concentrating on ideas becomes a habit, it will soon replace your old habit of reading words and sounds.

Repeating Exercises

For the maximum benefit, try to read each exercise in one sitting. But if you need to stop in the middle of an exercise because of a distraction, start over again at the beginning when you are ready to continue. The exercises are short enough that starting over should only take a little more time, but the best way to benefit is if you do the exercises long enough to stretch your reading muscles.

You might be concerned that starting an exercise over would distort your speed measurements because you would already be familiar with the material. It is true that you would most likely read faster the second time, but that concern misses the main purpose of the practice. Although an accurate measure of your reading speed may be useful feedback, the primary benefit comes from the practice itself.

Plus, there are other benefits to repeating an exercise. Rather than having an unfair advantage on the second reading, you will actually be further reinforcing your skills in new ways. You will be able to practice visualizing concepts faster the second time since it will be easier for you to come up with visuals, which will therefore allow you to more easily experience the type of reading you want to have, and to see what it feels like to fly over the words with excellent comprehension.

Free Progress Sheet Download

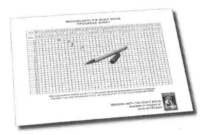

Here's an easy way to track and visualize your speed reading progress. This way you can easily track how you are doing over time. Download and print this free Progress Sheet. Simply mark an "X" in the box under the closest speed after each exercise. Each progress sheet has enough rows to record the speeds of 24 practice results.

Get this free download at: bit.ly/2bfdGpV

Don't be too concerned about your speed, or about bad habits such as regression or vocalizing. Just read through the text and let the special formatting guide your eyes to the meaningful phrases.

To determine your reading speed, measure the time it takes from start to finish and then use the formula below to calculate your words per minute. Since each exercise is exactly one thousand words long, the calculations will be simple and the results will be easy to compare.

Here's how you can calculate your WPM for these exercises:

Divide 60,000 by the number of seconds (60,000 / SECONDS)

Practice Exercise #1

The shift into higher reading speeds comes as a result of learning to read with the right brain, reading whole ideas rather than words. The methods and theories of this technique will be further explored throughout the book, but in this first practice segment, just pay attention to how the text is segregated into distinct and independently meaningful chunks of information. Without even trying, you should begin seeing phrases as whole ideas.

In this first exercise the text will be displayed in slightly shorter units of meaning than in the exercises that follow. The word-groups in this exercise will be no longer than three words each, to give you an easier introduction to reading word-groups.

As you begin this first exercise, do not be overly concerned with how you are reading. The black and gray highlighting should automatically guide you to the larger blocks of information. At this stage, just get used to seeing text divided into meaningful phrases.

When you come to the unaided portion of the text, try to continue seeing the words in meaningful groups on your own. Don't worry about exactly which words you group together, because there are no perfect groupings. Just try to continue seeing meaningful phrases, regardless of the phrase lengths you choose. What is most important is that the phrases make sense to you and are easy to imagine.

When you're ready, begin reading the first thousand words of

The Velveteen Rabbit by Margery Williams

The Velveteen Rabbit

There was once a velveteen rabbit, and in the beginning, he was really splendid. He was fat and bunchy, as a rabbit should be; his coat was spotted brown and white, he had real thread whiskers, and his ears were lined with pink sateen. On Christmas morning, when he sat wedged in the top of the Boy's stocking, with a sprig of holly between his paws, the effect was charming.

There were other things in the stocking, nuts and oranges and a toy engine, and chocolate almonds and a clockwork mouse, but the Rabbit was quite the best of all. For at least two hours the Boy loved him, and then Aunts and Uncles came to dinner, and there was a great rustling of tissue paper and unwrapping of parcels, and in the excitement of looking at all the new presents the Velveteen Rabbit was forgotten.

For a long time, he lived in the toy cupboard or on the nursery floor, and no one thought very much about him. He was naturally shy, and being only made of velveteen, some of the more expensive toys quite snubbed him. The mechanical toys were very superior, and looked down upon everyone else; they were full of modern ideas, and pretended they were real. The model boat, who had lived through two seasons and lost most of his paint, caught the tone from them and never missed an opportunity of referring to his rigging in technical terms.

The Rabbit could not claim to be a model of anything, for he didn't know that real rabbits existed; he thought they were all stuffed with sawdust like himself, and he understood that sawdust was quite out-of-date and should never be mentioned in modern circles. Even Timothy, the jointed wooden lion, who was made by the disabled soldiers, and should have had broader views, put on airs and pretended he was connected with Government. Between them all the poor little Rabbit was made to feel himself very insignificant and commonplace, and the only person who was kind to him at all was the Skin Horse.

The Skin Horse had lived longer in the nursery than any of the others. He was so old that his brown coat was bald in patches and showed the seams underneath, and most of the hairs in his tail had been pulled out to string bead necklaces. He was wise, for he had seen a long succession of mechanical toys arrive to boast and swagger, and by-and-by break their mainsprings and pass away, and he knew that they were only toys, and would never turn into anything else. For nursery magic is very strange and wonderful, and only those playthings that are old and wise and experienced like the Skin Horse understand all about it.

"What is REAL?" asked the Rabbit one day, when they were lying side by side near the nursery fender, before Nana came to tidy the room. "Does it mean having things that buzz inside you and a stick-out handle?"

"Real isn't how you are made," said the Skin Horse. "It's a thing that happens to you. When a child loves you for a long, long time, not just to play with, but REALLY loves you, then you become Real."

"Does it hurt?" asked the Rabbit.

"Sometimes," said the Skin Horse, for he was always truthful. "When you are Real you don't mind being hurt."

"Does it happen all at once, like being wound up," he asked, "or bit by bit?"

"It doesn't happen all at once," said the Skin Horse. "You become. It takes a long time. That's why it doesn't happen often to people who break easily, or have sharp edges, or who have to be carefully kept. Generally, by the time you are Real, most of your hair has been loved off, and your eyes drop out and you get loose in the joints and very shabby. But these things don't matter at all, because once you are Real you can't be ugly, except to people who don't understand."

"I suppose you are real?" said the Rabbit. And then he wished he had not said it, for he thought the Skin Horse might be sensitive. But the Skin Horse only smiled.

"The Boy's Uncle made me Real," he said. "That was a great many years ago; but once you are Real you can't become unreal again. It lasts for always."

The Rabbit sighed. He thought it would be a long time before this magic called Real happened to him. He longed to become Real, to know what it felt like; and yet the idea of growing shabby and losing his eyes and whiskers was rather sad. He wished that he could become it without these uncomfortable things happening to him.

There was a person called Nana who ruled the nursery. Sometimes she took no notice of the playthings lying about, and sometimes, for no reason whatever, she went swooping about like a great wind and hustled them away in cupboards. She called this "tidying up," and the playthings all hated it, especially the tin ones. The Rabbit didn't mind it so much, for wherever he was thrown he came down soft.

One evening, when the Boy was going to bed, he couldn't find the china dog that always slept with him. Nana was in a hurry, and it was too much trouble to hunt for china dogs at bedtime, so she simply looked about her, and seeing that the toy cupboard door stood open, she made a swoop.

"Here," she said, "take your old Bunny! He'll do to sleep with you!" And she dragged the Rabbit out by one ear, and put him into the Boy's arms.

That night, and for many nights after, the Velveteen Rabbit slept in the Boy's bed. At first he found it rather uncomfortable, for the Boy hugged him very tight, and sometimes he rolled over on him, and sometimes he pushed him so far under the pillow that the Rabbit could scarcely breathe. And he missed, too, those long moonlight hours in the nursery, when all the house was silent...

Chapter 2: How Can You Read Faster?

"I don't know, Marge... trying is the first step towards failure."
—*Homer Simpson*

Perhaps you've tried all the popular speed reading tricks:

- *Pushing your speed*
- *Trying not to verbalize*
- *Widening your eye span*
- *Using your finger as a pacer*
- *Ignoring "unimportant" words*
- *Making fewer eye stops per line*
- *Practicing moving your eyes faster*

But these haven't worked.

They might have temporarily increased your words per minute as you pushed yourself to read faster, but this increase was probably accompanied by a loss of comprehension. What good is that? If you read twice as fast but only understand half as much, you haven't gained a thing.

So, what can you do? How can you read faster and also maintain comprehension?

Sometimes the easiest way to find the solution to a problem is to make sure you are asking the right question to begin with. The right question can often be found by carefully determining what the real goal is.

What do you really want?

What you really want is to be able to pick up a book and understand what the author is saying in the least amount of time.

The key word is "understand." You are not just trying to finish the book faster; you are trying to collect *ideas*, to collect *experiences*, and to collect *information and knowledge*.

So the real question is...

"How can you *comprehend* faster?"

The answer to this question is what makes *Speed Reading with the Right Brain* different. This book is based on the principle that *comprehension must come first*, and therefore, using your right *conceptual* brain is key. The point of reading is to comprehend meaning, and the old methods that push you to see more words per minute miss that important point.

This book aims at a very specific target—the real act of reading. It is not about pre-reading, memorizing, or study habits. Instead, this book focuses specifically on what happens between the time the text enters your eyes as an image and when the information assimilates into your brain as knowledge.

Other skills—such as previewing, asking yourself questions, mind mapping, etc.—might be useful, but none of these are really about *reading*; they are about everything *around* reading. If you want to know more about these peripheral skills, there are abundant resources already available.

Speed Reading with the Right Brain is specifically about how to increase the speed of transferring ideas from the text to your brain. It focuses on how to read across each line of text, lock on to the information, and comprehend and assimilate this information into knowledge.

This book is NOT about pushing your reading speed, widening your eye-span, or suppressing bad reading habits. It is not another book of speed reading tips, tricks and "secrets." This book IS about learning to pay more attention to your reading.

Rather than eye exercises, this book focuses on exercising your mental processing, because reading is essentially a *mental* activity, not a *visual* one. Therefore, the instructions and exercises in this book are intended to strengthen your powers of concentration and focus.

The techniques and practice exercises in this book will show you how to read faster by comprehending faster. The way you'll do this is by learning to *conceptualize* your reading.

What is conceptualizing?

Read the phrase, *"the big black dog"* and concentrate on imagining what this group of words means. Imagine a big black dog, but don't only think of an image; think of what a big black dog means to *you*. Is it friendly? Is it scary? Is it beautiful? Is it smart? Do you remember any big black dogs?

Exactly what you imagine is not important—whatever pops into your head is OK; what *is* important is that what comes into your head is an *idea*, that you instantly imagine the meaning of the phrase. This is thinking *conceptually*.

This visual and conceptual concentration causes information to be passed to the right side of your brain, the side that specializes in the conceptual nature of ideas. It also connects the information to all the attributes—both visual and abstract—you associate this information with to create a larger, more complete idea of what the information means. The end result is a big-picture idea, the real essence of what the information means to you.

The right hemisphere of your brain has no verbal understanding. It can connect words with ideas, but it doesn't think in words. It does, however, have the powerful ability to imagine whole, complex ideas at once. This is how the right brain gives you clearer and faster comprehension, by processing information in larger and more meaningful chunks.

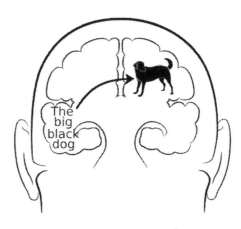

So far, this has been a basic introduction to conceptualizing, and there will be more discussion later about how to conceptualize different types of information. For now, realize that in order to conceptualize ideas, you'll need to be able to read *whole phrases* at a time, because there is seldom enough information in individual words to form meaningful mental concepts.

A short group of words, in the form of a meaningful phrase, can describe a complete, stand-alone idea. Phrases may be only a few words long, but together these few words can represent distinct pieces of information which can be easily imagined as whole units of meaning.

These meaningful pieces of text could be called "phrases," "word-groups," "clauses," "units of meaning," or "thought-units." But regardless of the label, they consist of any groups of words which represent whole ideas you can visualize or conceptualize.

Reading whole ideas increases your reading speed in two ways:

1. Concentrating on the bigger picture results in processing more meaningful information.
2. Taking in more words at a time results in reading more words per minute.

Reading whole phrases is like taking larger strides when you run. Switching from walking to running doesn't mean just moving your legs faster, but also lengthening your stride, thereby covering more distance with each step. This is basically how conceptualizing helps you read and comprehend faster, by letting you see a bigger picture and taking in larger blocks of information at a time.

In normal, unaided text, you have to perform both parts of this skill on your own. You have to concentrate on finding the meaningful word-groups, and at the same time, focus on the larger meaning of those word-groups. Trying to learn both parts of this skill together can be mentally overwhelming. It can be difficult to focus on meanings and concepts at the same time you are trying to select the meaningful word-groups.

But the formatted text in the exercises in this book will eliminate the work of finding phrases, allowing you to concentrate more attention on imagining the larger concepts. This makes it easy to practice reading in larger concepts. Then once you become familiar and comfortable with processing information in larger chunks, you will be able to pick out the phrases automatically on your own in normal, unformatted text.

Don't confuse reading phrases with the more common advice to make fewer eye-stops per line. Reading meaningful phrases is very different than simply trying to read in groups of some arbitrary number of words at a time. Instead, it is actively seeking conceptual units of information. In fact, it is this proactive, searching frame of mind which will make these word-groups automatically appear to you. This is because when you are aware that the information is in larger blocks of text, those blocks will become easier to recognize. Sentences are not smooth, consistent flows of evenly distributed information; they are more like clumps of ideas. Knowing this, and looking for these clumps, is what helps you see them.

As an example, consider this sentence:

It was a bright cold day in April, and the clocks were striking thirteen.

This should not be viewed as just a string of words, "*It—was—a—bright—cold—day—in—April,*" with each word adding just one more additional piece of information.

The sentence is actually better understood as *clumps* of ideas, "*It was—a bright cold day—in April,*" where each clump adds a specific and meaningful block of information to the sentence.

The exercises in this book identify these blocks of information for you. After practicing with these exercises, these meaningful phrases will automatically appear to you in regular text as you look for ideas and concepts. When you scan text for meaningful ideas, you will automatically focus on word-groups that represent the more complete and meaningful building blocks of the sentences—the separate ideas which can be imagined as pictures or concepts.

In the following demonstration, the meaningful phrases are indicated with black text. This example only shows one way this sentence could be divided; you could divide it differently as long as each phrase is meaningful to you on its own.

It was a bright cold day in April, and the clocks were striking thirteen.
It was **a bright cold day** in April, and the clocks were striking thirteen.
It was a bright cold day **in April,** and the clocks were striking thirteen.
It was a bright cold day in April, **and the clocks** were striking thirteen.
It was a bright cold day in April, and the clocks **were striking thirteen.**

As shown in this example, the first phrase you might lock onto could be "*It was.*" These two words can be imagined as a complete idea—in this case, one that gives you a context of the time this sentence is describing. So although "*It was*" is not something physical that you can actually form a picture of, it can still be imagined as a conceptual idea.

The next meaningful phrase could be "*a bright cold day;*" This time, the words create an idea that might be imagined as an actual picture.

As you continued across the sentence, you would pick up each of the short, independent ideas, quickly imagining what it means.

You can't know in advance which words will make up each phrase, but by looking for complete ideas, the meaningful portions will tend to jump out at you like friendly faces in a crowd. Also be aware that even though some word-groups may be more obvious than others, all these clumps of information will be easier to see when you are actively seeking ideas to visualize.

One other thing to consider is that this is not a conscious, mechanical process; you won't be thinking, "Look at the next word-group—now imagine the information." Instead, this will be an internalized, subconscious function that will take place automatically. You will concentrate only on looking for and imagining a flow of meaningful ideas, and your eyes and mind will automatically work together to discover them for you.

In short, the process of reading with the right brain consists of reading each sentence not as a list of individual words or as a string of sounds, but as a set of larger ideas which can then be linked together into the complete meaning of the entire sentence; this enables you to focus on the larger conceptual nature of what you are reading rather than the individual textual components.

More will be discussed later about reading word-groups and also about visualizing physical ideas versus conceptualizing abstract ideas, but for now just know that you will be focusing on larger, more meaningful pieces of information, and passing whole ideas to the conceptual right side of your brain for faster and more efficient processing.

As you practice with the specially formatted exercises in this book, you will experience what reading with the right brain feels like. You will experience reading and thinking in larger units of meaning and using the part of your brain which sees patterns and connections—the part which categorizes and understands larger concepts and connects them firmly with your existing knowledge.

Reading with the right brain will move you away from reading words and sounds, to reading *ideas*.

Practice Exercise #2

As you read the next exercise, look at each highlighted word-group all at once and not as a string of words. Look at each as a complete unit of meaning all its own. As you do, think of what it means or what it looks like. Take whatever quick mental snapshot that comes into your head for each phrase. As you focus on the whole meanings of entire phrases, you should feel the conceptual ideas expand into your right brain and float up into your consciousness.

If something is not easy to imagine as an actual picture or scene, at least conceptualize it and think of what it means. But remember, this is a fast and fleeting process, not a ponderous one. Quickly imagine each phrase and move on.

But, do not rush your reading. You mostly want to concentrate on involving the powerfully equipped parallel-processing visual machinery of your right hemisphere, to transfer the reading data from the wordy left side, through the thick bundle of nerves of the corpus callosum, and over to the right side for visualizing and conceptualizing. You want to experience what it feels like to "see" the meaning of what you read.

At first this may feel like it's causing your reading to slow down, but as your right brain starts to imagine what you are reading, your speed will increase on its own as the result of faster comprehension.

This next practice exercise will display phrases up to a maximum of four words long, but don't worry about this increase in the number of words per phrase; the reading process is the same, just with some slightly longer phrases. The actual number of words will be almost irrelevant when you concentrate on each phrase as a complete idea.

Even though you should be concentrating more on pushing your comprehension than on pushing your speed, you will still find it helpful to keep track of your words per minute. You will be glad you have this record for future comparisons.

And once again, do not be concerned with exactly how you group the words in the unaided section of the text. Just focus on seeing the larger meaningful ideas, and see which word-groups appear to you.

When you're ready, begin reading the first thousand words of

Pride and Prejudice by Jane Austen

Pride and Prejudice

It is a truth universally acknowledged that a single man in possession of a good fortune, must be in want of a wife.

However little known the feelings or views of such a man may be on his first entering a neighborhood, this truth is so well fixed in the minds of the surrounding families, that he is considered the rightful property of someone or other of their daughters.

"My dear Mr. Bennet," said his lady to him one day, "have you heard that Netherfield Park is let at last?"

Mr. Bennet replied that he had not.

"But it is," returned she; "for Mrs. Long has just been here, and she told me all about it."

Mr. Bennet made no answer.

"Do you not want to know who has taken it?" cried his wife impatiently.

"You want to tell me, and I have no objection to hearing it."

This was invitation enough.

"Why, my dear, you must know, Mrs. Long says that Netherfield is taken by a young man of large fortune from the north of England; that he came down on Monday in a chaise and four to see the place, and was so much delighted with it, that he agreed with Mr. Morris immediately; that he is to take possession before Michaelmas, and some of his servants are to be in the house by the end of next week."

"What is his name?"

"Bingley."

"Is he married or single?"

"Oh! Single, my dear, to be sure! A single man of large fortune; four or five thousand a year. What a fine thing for our girls!"

"How so? How can it affect them?"

"My dear Mr. Bennet," replied his wife, "how can you be so tiresome! You must know that I am thinking of his marrying one of them."

"Is that his design in settling here?"

"Design! Nonsense, how can you talk so! But it is very likely that he may fall in love with one of them, and therefore you must visit him as soon as he comes."

"I see no occasion for that. You and the girls may go, or you may send them by themselves, which perhaps will be still better, for as you are as handsome as any of them, Mr. Bingley may like you the best of the party."

"My dear, you flatter me. I certainly have had my share of beauty, but I do not pretend to be anything extraordinary now. When a woman has five grown-up daughters, she ought to give over thinking of her own beauty."

"In such cases, a woman has not often much beauty to think of."

"But, my dear, you must indeed go and see Mr. Bingley when he comes into the neighborhood."

"It is more than I engage for, I assure you."

"But consider your daughters. Only think what an establishment it would be for one of them. Sir William and Lady Lucas are determined to go, merely on that account, for in general, you know, they visit no newcomers. Indeed, you must go, for it will be impossible for us to visit him if you do not."

"You are over-scrupulous, surely. I dare say Mr. Bingley will be very glad to see you; and I will send a few lines by you to assure him of my hearty consent to his marrying whichever he chooses of the girls; though I must throw in a good word for my little Lizzy."

"I desire you will do no such thing. Lizzy is not a bit better than the others; and I am sure she is not half so handsome as Jane, nor half so good-humored as Lydia. But you are always giving her the preference."

"They have none of them much to recommend them," replied he; "they are all silly and ignorant like other girls; but Lizzy has something more of quickness than her sisters."

"Mr. Bennet, how can you abuse your own children in such a way? You take delight in vexing me. You have no compassion for my poor nerves."

"You mistake me, my dear. I have a high respect for your nerves. They are my old friends. I have heard you mention them with consideration these last twenty years at least."

"Ah, you do not know what I suffer."

"But I hope you will get over it, and live to see many young men of four thousand a year, come into the neighborhood."

"It will be no use to us, if twenty such should come, since you will not visit them."

"Depend upon it, my dear, that when there are twenty, I will visit them all."

Mr. Bennet was so odd a mixture of quick parts, sarcastic humor, reserve, and caprice, that the experience of three-and-twenty years had been insufficient to make his wife understand his character. Her mind was less difficult to develop. She was a woman of mean understanding, little information, and uncertain temper. When she was discontented, she fancied herself nervous. The business of her life was to get her daughters married; its solace was visiting and news.

Mr. Bennet was among the earliest of those who waited on Mr. Bingley. He had always intended to visit him, though to the last always assuring his wife that he should not go; and till the evening after the visit was paid she had no knowledge of it. It was then disclosed in the following manner. Observing his second daughter employed in trimming a hat, he suddenly addressed her with:

"I hope Mr. Bingley will like it, Lizzy."

"We are not in a way to know what Mr. Bingley likes," said her mother resentfully, "since we are not to visit."

"But you forget, Mamma," said Elizabeth, "that we shall meet him at the assemblies, and that Mrs. Long promised to introduce him."

"I do not believe Mrs. Long will do any such thing. She has two nieces of her own. She is a selfish, hypocritical woman, and I have no opinion of her."

"No more have I," said Mr. Bennet; "and I am glad to find that you do not depend on her serving you."

Mrs. Bennet deigned not to make any reply, but, unable to contain herself, began scolding one of her daughters.

"Don't keep coughing so, Kitty, for Heaven's sake! Have a little compassion...

Chapter 3: Your New Reading Experience

Words are flowing out like
Endless rain into a paper cup.
They slither wildly as they slip away
across the universe.
- "Across the Universe," the Beatles

There certainly does seem to be an endless flow of words today. Unlike a short time ago, when our access to words was limited to the space available on our bookshelves or to the amount of time we could spend in our local library, today we have literally an infinite amount of reading material available. It's easier than ever to access, and it's there for us twenty-four hours a day. Our biggest challenges now are deciding what to read and how to get through it all.

Today there really is only one limit to the information available, and that limit is us. Our reading speed is the only limit there is to the many things we can know and the many stories we can experience.

A superior reading skill can give us greater access to this expanding cornucopia of information, and access to this information can have a powerful effect on our lives. It can make our lives easier, happier, and even safer and healthier—which might even mean longer! Plus, this greater access to information will also make our lives more interesting, as well as make *us* more interesting.

In addition to acquiring information, improved reading skills can even physically enhance our brains. A study in the proceedings of the National Academy of Sciences found that older people who read regularly are two and a half times less likely to have Alzheimer's disease. Reading skills also strengthen our brains by boosting memory, focus, concentration, and analytical thinking.

But wait, there's more! Conceptualizing information and really paying attention to its meaning will increase your *awareness* of life. Instead of having a superficial awareness of the things you see, hear, and read—

41

conceptual thinking will make you more aware of the deeper reality of what things actually mean.

Your Reading Upgrade

Conceptualizing ideas instead of listening to sounds is learning to experience reading in a new way. This is a major upgrade to those very old reading lessons from your childhood.

Remember when you first learned to read? You learned all the letters and the sounds the letters made, and then you also learned when the letters made different sounds in different words. It was all pretty confusing at first—a lot for a little kid to take in—but eventually you learned to read.

Some really helpful tools during that learning process were the special reading books, the *Dick and Jane* stories. These books were carefully developed to make learning as easy and interesting as possible. By practicing with these books, something gradually happened—you began to recognize words at a glance without thinking of each letter. At that point, reading became automatic; you could read words without thinking about how you did it.

That's about as far as your reading education went; you could read *words*. Today you're no longer reading about Dick and Jane. You've got a lot more to read now, and that reading has gotten a lot more sophisticated and complicated. But when was your last reading lesson? Fifth grade? Today, are you reading any better than a fifth grader?

For a lot of people, the answer is, sadly, "No." This is not a happy group of people because it's frustrating to have poor reading skills, and it's embarrassing, too. It's frustrating to take forever to read a single book, and it's embarrassing to be uninformed about so many of the interesting and fast changing events in the world.

The Unread Masses

Unfortunately, poor readers aren't a lonely bunch; they have a lot more company than good readers have. There are sadly more and more people who, for one reason or another, have either not progressed in their reading skills after childhood, or have even regressed through a lack of practice. Sure they may read their text messages and tweets, and maybe even headlines and picture captions, but a large number of people shy away from anything more demanding than the *TV Guide*, and they restrict the selection of what they read to material with plenty of pictures. At a time when there is more information than ever easily available to us, we are nonetheless turning into a readerless society.

Here are some sad reading statistics. Although the numbers are staggering, they are unfortunately not that shocking.

- 58% of the US adult population never reads another book after high school.
- 42% of college students never read another book after college.
- 80% of US families did not buy or read a book last year.
- 70% of US adults have not been to a bookstore in the last five years.
- 57% of new books are not read to completion.
- Most readers do not get past page 18 in a book they have purchased.

Benefits

I know the lament: "Who's got time?" Of course we're all so busy, and reading takes SO MUCH TIME! So it comes down to a cost-benefit analysis: How much time will these improved reading skills cost, and how much benefit will be received? The benefit is that you will get more out of your reading; enjoy it more, be more informed, and have better comprehension and retention. However, the real price is actually free, because with faster reading, your time investment will be continually refunded.

Time

How much time does it take to read a book? Remember that the average adult reads two hundred words per minute. Assume this average person wants to read a book which is three hundred pages long and has approximately four hundred words per page. This book would then have a total of one hundred twenty thousand words. At two hundred words per minute, this book would take ten hours to read (120,000 / 200 = 600 minutes or 10 hours). At four hundred words per minute, however, this book would only take half that time—five hours.

So, how long would it take this average person learn to increase his reading speed from reading two hundred words per minute to four hundred? Four hundred words per minute is not actually a very difficult speed to reach. If it took a total of five hours of practice to learn this speed increase, then those five hours would be saved back after reading only one book. But a reading speed increase is a gift that keeps on giving, because the faster a person reads, the more books they will want to read and therefore, the more time they will get back.

Besides this time rebate, what about the benefits side of the equation? The major benefit, of course, is improved comprehension. This means getting more *out* of your reading. When someone asks, "What is that book about?" you can actually tell him.

But there are even more benefits to gain from improved reading skills.

Power

The mental exercise of reading develops a more powerful mind. The act of reading is one of the most sophisticated mental achievements of the human mind. The mental exercise this involves strengthens your intelligence, sharpens your analytical skills, and improves your ability to separate reality from fiction.

Even more power can be developed by extending your reading to your right brain. One way is by improving the power of your memory. By conceptualizing phrases, you are concentrating on more complex ideas, making your reading more memorable and storing information more efficiently. You are not just reading new information, but conceptualizing it and associating it with previous information. Each of these complex memories creates even more association points for future memories to attach to. The more you know, the easier it becomes to know more. And more knowledge is more power.

Success

Reading—combined with the ability to understand, recall, and make use of the material you have read—also plays a major role in achieving success in life.

Faster reading and better comprehension have powerful impacts; whether it's being better informed in your job, or having a better understanding of your studies, or simply by being a more well-rounded and informed conversationalist.

Good reading skills produce many advantages. It's no exaggeration to say that in this modern interconnected and competitive world, the ability to read, comprehend, and better organize information into useful knowledge could be considered tantamount to a survival skill, and a prerequisite to most success.

Uniqueness

By concentrating on concepts, you will be remembering not just the facts, but the real meaning behind what you read as well. You can't remember every detail you read, but you can remember the *meaning*. Your own personal meaning is created by the selection and significance of attributes you connect to information—these selections being based primarily on your previous knowledge and interests.

These conceptual connections are what make each of us unique. Each person has his own informational combinations, and these combinations and intersections of information create each person's uniqueness, enabling each person to see information in unique ways with unique perspectives.

This is true of all kinds of reading. No matter what you read, all reading changes you. In a lot of ways, we are what we read. We are the sum of these experiences, and many of our experiences come to us vicariously through reading, from anywhere and from any-when. Regardless of whether it is fact or fiction, educational or relaxation, all reading adds something to who we are, and to our own uniqueness.

Innovation

It's the conceptual connections of information which create the real power of human intelligence. The information itself is cheap—the whole world of information is only a Google search away. The real power of human intelligence is not in the collection of information, but in the *connections* of information. It is at these unique intersections that ideas build upon each other to produce new, relevant and more valuable ideas. These unique combinations are the real mother of innovation.

Read for Enjoyment

Many people who say they don't have time to read will also say they don't have time to learn to read faster, but since reading faster could *save* them time, this seems like a contradiction.

When you are facing a contradiction, check your premises; you will usually find that one of them is wrong. I believe the mistaken premise here the belief that those people *want* to read in the first place.

I suspect the real truth is that most people don't want to read simply because it's not enjoyable for them. I hope one benefit of conceptual reading is to make reading more enjoyable. I have found that by improving my own reading, I've developed what feels almost like a reading addiction. The more I read, the more I learn; the more I learn, the more things I discover that I want to read about.

So why not deemphasize the collection of raw data, and instead concentrate on the development of intelligence by fostering your reasoning ability and creativity—which are all enhanced through the connectedness of information and conceptual reading of ideas?

Realistic Expectations

Of course every skill takes practice, but at least this is practice that works. This is not practicing some so-called secret speed reading tricks—like the ones you find in every other book. This is practicing seeing the ideas behind the words by concentrating on the larger blocks of information.

But let's be realistic—there are a lot of very unbelievable claims being made in the speed reading industry. You're probably suspicious of many of them, or you at least suspect they might be too good to be true.

Instead of filling your head with nonsense, I want to give you something that will truly be of value to you. Forget all the exercises that focus on eye movement. Instead, focus on thinking conceptually about what you are reading by employing the right side of your brain to see the big picture, the whole idea of what you read.

With the explosion of information available through e-readers and the internet, we are likely witnessing a fundamental transformation of the world. In fact, we are probably at the beginning of an unprecedented information and knowledge revolution—a quantum leap in the development of human intelligence and potential. The driver of this change is the worldwide connectedness and collaboration that has suddenly been made available through the internet.

All of this change, however, depends on reading. A rocket ship is about to take off, headed for the future, but only those with excellent reading skills will be aboard.

Practice Exercise #3

As you practice this exercise, keep in mind that there is still a speed below which we tend to vocalize the words, at least internally, just because we're bored. If you are careful to read slightly faster while concentrating on imagining the meaning of what you read, there therefore will be less of a tendency to say the words.

During this exercise, try to visualize in your imagination what you are reading. Visualizing ideas also has a powerful effect on silencing your inner voice since it's actually difficult to verbalize while concentrating on visuals. It seems that concentrating on one makes it harder to do the other, so you don't need to make any special effort to silence that voice; just concentrate on the visuals but avoid going too slowly.

This, and all remaining exercises, will have a maximum phrase length of five words. You should have no problem picking up these larger phrases because each will still represent only a single idea. In fact, you may find that you can read even faster with larger phrases because you will be covering more text per glance. But don't push your speed past your comprehension; focus on imagining what each phrase means and the speed will come.

Once you've finished reading the exercise, make a note of your speed result for future comparisons.

When you're ready, begin reading the first thousand words of

The Picture of Dorian Gray by Oscar Wilde

The Picture of Dorian Gray

The studio was filled with the rich odor of roses, and when the light summer wind stirred amidst the trees of the garden, there came through the open door the heavy scent of the lilac, or the more delicate perfume of the pink-flowering thorn.

From the corner of the divan of Persian saddle-bags on which he was lying, smoking, as was his custom, innumerable cigarettes, Lord Henry Wotton could just catch the gleam of the honey-sweet and honey-colored blossoms of a laburnum, whose tremulous branches seemed hardly able to bear the burden of a beauty so flame-like as theirs; and now and then the fantastic shadows of birds in flight flitted across the long tussore-silk curtains that were stretched in front of the huge window, producing a kind of momentary Japanese effect, and making him think of those pallid, jade-faced painters of Tokyo who, through the medium of an art that is necessarily immobile, seek to convey the sense of swiftness and motion. The sullen murmur of the bees shouldering their way through the long unmown grass, or circling with monotonous insistence round the dusty gilt horns of the straggling woodbine, seemed to make the stillness more oppressive. The dim roar of London was like the bourdon note of a distant organ.

In the center of the room, clamped to an upright easel, stood the full-length portrait of a young man of extraordinary personal beauty, and in front of it, some little distance away, was sitting the artist himself, Basil Hallward, whose sudden disappearance some years ago caused, at the time, such public excitement and gave rise to so many strange conjectures.

As the painter looked at the gracious and comely form he had so skillfully mirrored in his art, a smile of pleasure passed across his face, and seemed about to linger there. But he suddenly started up, and closing his eyes, placed his fingers upon the lids, as though he sought to imprison within his brain some curious dream from which he feared he might awake.

"It is your best work, Basil, the best thing you have ever done," said Lord Henry languidly. "You must certainly send it next year to the Grosvenor. The Academy is too large and too vulgar. Whenever I have gone there, there have been either so many people that I have not been able to see the pictures, which was dreadful, or so many pictures that I have not been able to see the people, which was worse. The Grosvenor is really the only place."

"I don't think I shall send it anywhere," he answered, tossing his head back in that odd way that used to make his friends laugh at him at Oxford. "No, I won't send it anywhere."

Lord Henry elevated his eyebrows and looked at him in amazement through the thin blue wreaths of smoke that curled up in such fanciful whorls from his heavy, opium-tainted cigarette. "Not send it anywhere? My dear fellow, why? Have you any reason? What odd chaps you painters are! You do anything in the world to gain a reputation. As soon as you have one, you seem to want to throw it away. It is silly of you, for there is only one thing in the world worse than being talked about, and that is not being talked about. A portrait like this would set you far above all the young men in England, and make the old men quite jealous, if old men are ever capable of any emotion."

"I know you will laugh at me," he replied, "but I really can't exhibit it. I have put too much of myself into it."

Lord Henry stretched himself out on the divan and laughed.

"Yes, I knew you would; but it is quite true, all the same."

"Too much of yourself in it! Upon my word, Basil, I didn't know you were so vain; and I really can't see any resemblance between you, with your rugged strong face and your coal-black hair, and this young Adonis, who looks as if he was made out of ivory and rose-leaves. Why, my dear Basil, he is a Narcissus, and you—well, of course you have an intellectual expression and all that. But beauty, real beauty, ends where an intellectual expression begins. Intellect is in itself a mode of exaggeration, and destroys the harmony of any face. The moment one sits down to think, one becomes all nose, or all forehead, or something horrid. Look at the successful men in any of the learned professions. How perfectly hideous they are! Except, of course, in the Church. But then in the Church they don't think. A bishop keeps on saying at the age of eighty what he was told to say when he was a boy of eighteen, and as a natural consequence he always looks absolutely delightful. Your mysterious young friend, whose name you have never told me, but whose picture really fascinates me, never thinks. I feel quite sure of that. He is some brainless beautiful creature who should be always here in winter when we have no flowers to look at, and always here in summer when we want something to chill our intelligence. Don't flatter yourself, Basil: you are not in the least like him."

"You don't understand me, Harry," answered the artist. "Of course I am not like him. I know that perfectly well. Indeed, I should be sorry to look like him. You shrug your shoulders? I am telling you the truth. There is a fatality about all physical and intellectual distinction, the sort of fatality that seems to dog through history the faltering steps of kings. It is better not to be different from one's fellows. The ugly and the stupid have the best of it in this world. They can sit at their ease and gape at the play. If they know nothing of victory, they are at least spared the knowledge of defeat. They live as well as...

Chapter 4: The Basics

Many people seem to be looking for a quick and easy way to read faster—some kind of ninja trick or magic beans. This preference for a "magical" solution is clearly evidenced by the popularity of books with titles promising to teach you speed reading in one hour or less.

The hidden truth behind such promises is that when they say "Learn to Speed Read in One Hour," they're not actually promising to teach you TO READ faster in one hour; they're only promising to teach you HOW TO read faster. There is a subtle but important difference; the "one hour'" only refers to how long it will take you to read their little book! At the end of the hour, you still won't be able to read any faster; you'll just know *how* (supposedly) to *begin* learning.

If you only want to know *how to* read faster, I can tell you in just a few seconds:

3 Mind Tricks to Power-Up Your Reading

1. Read meaningful groups of words at a time.
2. Concentrate on whole ideas instead of words.
3. Conceptualize the meanings of those ideas.

This can even be further shortened to simply: ***Conceptualize*** the ***ideas*** of ***meaningful word-groups.***

That's it; the rest takes practice. Simply put, reading faster requires comprehending faster.

That's *how* you do it, but of course the only way to turn knowledge into skill is by doing. But although there is practice required, I promise I'm not going to waste your time with a bunch of strange and impractical exercises. You won't be asked to dwell on things that don't work, don't interest you, and don't make sense. Instead, the specially formatted practice exercises are a kind of rapid immersion into reading for ideas.

But please do me a favor...

Forget your dreams of becoming the next Kim Peek. You've probably heard of incredible savants like Mr. Peek, amazing people who can read thousands of words per minute. Very few people are savants, and I would think few would want to be. These rare people are not what they may seem. They can "read" at astonishing speeds—often even remembering every word—but the fact is, they usually don't understand what they've read. They may be able to recite every word of a book, but they can't actually have a conversation about it. In this way, they are a bit like human computers: all speed and memory, but no comprehension.

The goal of this book is not to make you a savant, but to give you something valuable and honest, the ability to get more out of what you read—in less time—by *improving your comprehension*.

So, how do you improve your comprehension? The answer is surprisingly and almost deceptively simple: by *improving your thinking*.

Strangely, the thinking part of reading is often taken for granted. People frequently imagine that learning to read simply involves learning how to recognize written words, but words are practically meaningless without the context of their surrounding words.

Not until you think about what whole groups of words mean does text become ideas and raw data becomes meaningful information. "Thinking" is what happens when data is conceptualized—when it is classified, categorized, filtered, and evaluated as to what it means to *you*. When you conceptualize the ideas of meaningful word-groups, you translate the text from words into information. And when this information is associated with previous information, it becomes new knowledge by modifying your existing information.

So let's explore what these three "reading tricks" mean.

Trick 1 - Read Meaningful Groups of Words at a Time

To understand faster, you will need to read whole groups of words at a time. And in order to understand word-groups at a glance, these must be groups of words which form independently meaningful ideas on their own. But you already do this.

Reading multiple words at once is not a new idea. For example, before 1940, the word "percent" was more commonly written, and understood, as two words: "per" and "cent."

Today, "percent" is not only considered one word, but a single, unified idea as well. The two ideas, "per" as *for each* and "cent" as *one hundredth*, were combined into a new larger and more complex idea. After constant and regular use together, the two words gradually became accepted as one word, "percent," with one meaning, *for each one hundredth*. Joining these words meant more than just omitting the space between them; it meant actually beginning to think of this word-group as a separate, uniquely distinct idea of its own.

This is the same way many compound words were created—they started as separate words and became meaningful word-groups. The words were combined because it was easier and faster to think of them as single, complete concepts.

So we've always combined meaningful word-groups. Now, we are taking it to the next level by combining even more words. Just as you can immediately understand the whole concept of a compound word—such as "**forever**" (1890), "**nearby**" (1925), or "**worthwhile**" (1960)—you can also instantly imagine the concept of a multi-word thought unit—such as "**for-a-while**," "**near-my-house**," or "**worth-your-time**."

The point is, it has always been possible to read words together as long as the word-groups formed meaningful ideas; reading phrases is just a further extension of this process of thinking and communicating in larger, more complex—and thereby more efficient—conceptual ideas.

Trick 2 - Concentrate on Whole Ideas Instead of Words

The only way to be able to understand word-groups at a glance is to think of them as ideas rather than just words.

You can't *say* two words at the same time because it's not possible to pronounce words simultaneously, one on top of the other. Even if you could, it would not be possible to understand the resulting cacophony. Likewise, it's also not possible to *think* of separate words simultaneously.

But it *is* possible to think of complete and more complex ideas—single thoughts represented by groups of words—all at once. In fact, it's even easier to imagine the meaning of such word-groups, because their combined information is more specific. For example, "driving rain" is more specific and easier to imagine than just the words "driving" or "rain" alone. The single words "driving" or "rain," without the context of supporting information, are so vague as to make it almost impossible to know what to imagine. Words have definitions, but real meaning is determined by the way multiple words are put together.

The information from a single word is so small and vague that it is usually difficult for our minds to know what to do with it before we connect it with its neighboring words. A meaningful word-group though is much easier and quicker to imagine and understand.

The larger ideas represented by groups of words are not only easier to imagine, but they are also easier to connect to our previous knowledge, making for stronger and longer lasting memories. These word-groups are easier to connect because they have more potential connection points due to the larger number of attributes each of them contains.

For instance, consider the two words "red" and "cat." "Red" can connect to our knowledge of colors, and "cat" can connect to our knowledge of animals.

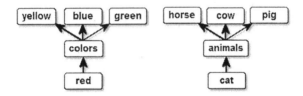

But "red cat" taken as one complete thought—even though it is only two words long—can connect to both *colors* AND *animals*. These extra connection points make this larger, more complex idea *stickier*, which makes it faster to imagine and easier to remember. When you think of "red cat," your mind can associate it with red things as well as with animals.

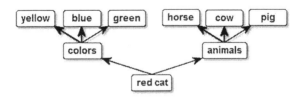

Of course, this example has been intentionally over-simplified to make a point. There are actually many possible connections for either "red" or "cat." For example, "red" can be associated with bright things or danger. And "cat" can be associated with furry things or pets. Furthermore, by considering "red cat" as a complete thought, you also introduce additional points of contact, such as unusual cats (because red is an unusual color for a cat) and unusual red things. The larger and more complex an idea, the more ways you will have to remember it and the more things it will remind you of.

The main point here is that larger, more complex ideas have many more possible points of contact in your mind. Think of those stubborn little burrs that get stuck in your socks—the more points they have, the easier they stick and the longer they hang on.

Trick 3 - Conceptualize the Meaning of These Ideas

This is a simple, yet powerful trick to get your right hemisphere involved. By conceptualizing ideas, you force your mind into a conceptual thinking mode. When you see a phrase—for example "the fat blue dog"—and you conceptualize this by imagining it as an image, the image will cause several more neurons to fire than would have if you had only thought of the words and their sounds. Your mind will also instantly pay more attention because humans are very visual animals and images are what our brains crave most.

Please note that I will often use the words "conceptualizing" and "visualizing" interchangeably. There will be more discussion of these terms later, but the basically, visualizing is a subset of conceptualizing, and because of this relationship, doing one often leads to the other.

Now, although conceptualizing is actually a simple trick, it may not seem so simple to actually sustain at first, and you may feel yourself going into and out of the conceptualizing zone. Here's why:

When you visualize the meaning of phrases, the ideas will seem to leap off the page and into your mind as your right brain focuses on the conceptual nature of the information. However, it takes practice to learn to "see" ideas as you read, and at first this process may slow your reading. You may then become impatient and be tempted to return to your old way of reading—by simply connecting text to matching words and sounds. And if you get frustrated and skip visualizing one phrase, it makes it harder to visualize the next one, and then the next. You will lose your connection with the material, but you will still be tempted to keep reading along anyway, without visualizing and without *comprehending*.

This type of mental "blanking out" is an important thing to understand. It happens often in reading, and it's necessary to consider the cause in order to prevent it. It isn't that you are not paying enough attention or concentrating hard enough. The problem is that your chain of comprehension becomes broken when you skip a piece of information.

Imagine your concentration as an airplane trying to take off. But the engine begins to sputter—first once, then a few times. Each time the engine misfires makes it harder to get off the ground, and as long as this happens, it will never gain enough power to become airborne. If it can gain enough speed to liftoff, then staying airborne will be relatively easy.

Similarly, each time your concentration misfires, it also loses power. It takes discipline and effort to conceptually visualize what you are reading, but this visualizing will get your powerful right brain involved in reading and lift your reading into the higher conceptual comprehension necessary for faster reading. This participation of your right hemisphere will also make your reading come more alive as you begin seeing the larger conceptual nature of the ideas you are reading.

The act of using your visual right hemisphere will also cause you to direct additional mental attention to the information, and it will cause you to filter out more distractions. The text will also become more meaningful since even attempting to visualize forces you to actually *think* about what the text means.

At this point, we have mostly considered visual imagery, but visualizing pictures is only one form of conceptualizing. We will get more into other types of conceptualizing later, including how to conceptualize unobservable ideas, but for now at least make sure to actively *think* about what you're reading. Instead of your consciousness just sitting back and listening to you read it a story, you will use conceptual images to wake it up and say, "Pay attention. This is important."

Keep These Tips in Mind

- Visualize. The brain is wired to notice and react more quickly and emotionally to visuals.
- Phrases are ideas, not sounds; think about what they *mean.*
- Words in phrases give each other context and become more meaningful. Looking for that meaning will help you to see those word-groups.
- If at times you get stuck and lose concentration, stop focusing on speed. Refocus on ideas by forcing your brain to visualize. Concentrate on comprehension and the speed will come.

The suggestions in this book may appear unusual to some people, but have you noticed that the other methods aren't working? Learning to read phrases is as simple as it is uncommon; it's a simple *uncommon-*sense solution to reading more efficiently, effectively, powerfully, and quickly.

I've already mentioned that this takes practice, but you would be surprised how many people give up when they discover practice is required. Another group quits when they find it will take longer than an hour. I wish I could help these people, but the subjects of tenacity and persistence would be a whole other book. However, with proper practice and technique, you will see positive results. It may seem difficult at first, but this is really just actively *thinking* about what you read.

Keywords

Another helpful thing to notice is that the last word is often the "key" word in each meaningful phrase. It's like the other words in the phrase were leading up this this word. Focusing on these key words can make your reading smoother as you more quickly zoom in on the main idea of each phrase.

As you practice reading phrases, you will develop the right-brained habit of creating visual and conceptual representations of what you read. This alone will make your reading flow more smoothly, as you read with a deeper and more conceptual understanding, and you *experience* the text rather than just listen to it.

But even though you are conceptualizing each phrase as a meaningful idea, these individual phrases do not stand alone. Each phrase is still a link within the larger meaning of a whole sentence. As you conceptualize phrases, you must also link them together as interlocking bricks into the completed structure of the whole sentence.

Looking at these keywords is one way to pull the phrases together. This does not mean ignoring other words. It just means paying special attention to words that describe who or what is involved, or what is happening. For example, here is a sentence divided into phrases and with possible key words underlined.

<u>Dorothy</u> lived in the <u>midst</u> of the <u>great</u> Kansas <u>prairies</u>, with Uncle <u>Henry</u>, who was a <u>farmer</u>, and Aunt <u>Em</u>, who <u>was</u> the farmer's <u>wife</u>.

Even though you are reading this sentence in meaningful phrases, there are certain words which represent the overall direction and framework of the sentence. You can't skip or ignore any words, but these key words will give you a very good idea of what the sentence is about. Paying special attention to these will increase your comprehension and reading speed because these words will tie the phrases together and add an overall structure to the sentence.

There are no exact rules of grammar for selecting these key words, but they are usually the subjects and verbs of the sentence. They are also—as in the example above—quite often the first word of the sentence and then the *last* word in each phrase.

However, just as the word-groups you select don't have to be perfect, neither do the keywords—they just have to work. You are simply focusing on the words that act as a summary to the sentence.

This may seem like a lot to think about while reading, but it is only another helpful tool for focusing on ideas versus words. With practice, the habit of seeing text as larger meaningful ideas should become internalized and unconscious and assist in making the most use of our finite amounts of cognitive energy.

Practice Exercise #4

As you do the practice exercises, remember that speed is the result of better comprehension. Bring each phrase into clear focus by visualizing or conceptualizing its meaning, and let the speed increase as a natural result. You don't want to feel like you are *pushing* your speed, but rather *pulling* it along behind your faster, more powerful comprehension.

One more suggestion—besides practicing with the exercises, you should start to apply reading phrases to your regular reading. In fact, there is no reason not to apply this method to the regular text portions of this book. Just remember not to go faster than you can comprehend, and remember to not include too many words at in each phrase; smaller phrases are easier to quickly imagine while you are learning.

When you're ready, begin reading the first thousand words of

The War of the Worlds by H. G. Wells

The War of the Worlds

No one would have believed in the last years of the nineteenth century that this world was being watched keenly and closely by intelligences greater than man's and yet as mortal as his own; that as men busied themselves about their various concerns they were scrutinized and studied, perhaps almost as narrowly as a man with a microscope might scrutinize the transient creatures that swarm and multiply in a drop of water. With infinite complacency men went to and fro over this globe about their little affairs, serene in their assurance of their empire over matter. It is possible that the infusoria under the microscope do the same. No one gave a thought to the older worlds of space as sources of human danger, or thought of them only to dismiss the idea of life upon them as impossible or improbable. It is curious to recall some of the mental habits of those departed days. At most terrestrial men fancied there might be other men upon Mars, perhaps inferior to themselves and ready to welcome a missionary enterprise. Yet across the gulf of space, minds that are to our minds as ours are to those of the beasts that perish, intellects vast and cool and unsympathetic, regarded this earth with envious eyes, and slowly and surely drew their plans against us. And early in the twentieth century, came the great disillusionment.

The planet Mars, I scarcely need remind the reader, revolves about the sun at a mean distance of 140,000,000 miles, and the light and heat it receives from the sun is barely half of that received by this world. It must be, if the nebular hypothesis has any truth, older than our world; and long before this earth ceased to be molten, life upon its surface must have begun its course. The fact that it is scarcely one seventh of the volume of the earth must have accelerated its cooling to the temperature at which life could begin. It has air and water and all that is necessary for the support of animated existence.

Yet so vain is man, and so blinded by his vanity, that no writer, up to the very end of the nineteenth century, expressed any idea that intelligent life might have developed there far, or indeed at all, beyond its earthly level. Nor was it generally understood that since Mars is older than our earth, with scarcely a quarter of the superficial area and remoter from the sun, it necessarily follows that it is not only more distant from time's beginning but nearer its end.

The secular cooling that must someday overtake our planet has already gone far indeed with our neighbor. Its physical condition is still largely a mystery, but we know now that even in its equatorial region the midday temperature barely approaches that of our coldest winter. Its air is much more attenuated than ours, its oceans have shrunk until they cover but a third of its surface, and as its slow seasons change huge snowcaps gather and melt about either pole and periodically inundate its temperate zones. That last stage of exhaustion, which to us is still incredibly remote, has become a present-day problem for the inhabitants of Mars. The immediate pressure of necessity has brightened their intellects, enlarged their powers, and hardened their hearts. And looking across space with instruments, and intelligences such as we have scarcely dreamed of, they see, at its nearest distance only 35,000,000 of miles sunward of them, a morning star of hope, our own warmer planet, green with vegetation and grey with water, with a cloudy atmosphere eloquent of fertility, with glimpses through its drifting cloud wisps of broad stretches of populous country and narrow, navy-crowded seas.

And we men, the creatures who inhabit this earth, must be to them at least as alien and lowly as are the monkeys and lemurs to us. The intellectual side of man already admits that life is an incessant struggle for existence, and it would seem that this too is the belief of the minds upon Mars. Their world is far gone in its cooling and this world is still crowded with life, but crowded only with what they regard as inferior animals. To carry warfare sunward is, indeed, their only escape from the destruction that, generation after generation, creeps upon them.

And before we judge of them too harshly we must remember what ruthless and utter destruction our own species has wrought, not only upon animals, such as the vanished bison and the dodo, but upon its inferior races. The Tasmanians, in spite of their human likeness, were entirely swept out of existence in a war of extermination waged by European immigrants, in the space of fifty years. Are we such apostles of mercy as to complain if the Martians warred in the same spirit?

The Martians seem to have calculated their descent with amazing subtlety—their mathematical learning is evidently far in excess of ours—and to have carried out their preparations with a well-nigh perfect unanimity. Had our instruments permitted it, we might have seen the gathering trouble far back in the nineteenth century. Men like Schiaparelli watched the red planet—it is odd, by-the-bye, that for countless centuries Mars has been the star of war—but failed to interpret the fluctuating appearances of the markings they mapped so well. All that time the Martians must have been getting ready.

During the opposition of 1894 a great light was seen on the illuminated part of the disk, first at the Lick Observatory, then by Perrotin of Nice, and then by other observers. English readers heard of it first in the issue of Nature dated August 2...

Chapter 5: Skills

Every skill requires practice, but some strategies exist that can boost any practice to maximum effectiveness—and some of these strategies are especially suited to reading skills. A little consideration of these strategies before continuing with the exercises will be time well-spent.

Force vs. Technique

Watch students of martial arts, and you will often see them practicing their moves in slow motion. It doesn't look very powerful because they are moving so slowly, but what they are doing is perfecting their form and improving their technique. They know that power comes more from technique than from physical force. This same principle of technique over force applies to reading.

Instead of the brute force method of simply trying to push yourself to read faster, real reading power can be achieved by concentrating on techniques to learn to read text as a flow of ideas rather than a string of words. It's mastering this skill that gives power to your reading. If learning a physical skill like martial arts requires careful attention to technique, then it shouldn't be surprising that this is also true of something as complex as reading.

Practice

"Practice does not make perfect. Only perfect practice makes perfect."
—Vince Lombardi

Practice only creates *habits*, and these habits can be good, bad, or mediocre. Therefore, the type of practice you choose to engage in is much more important than the amount.

Consider the skill of typing as an example. When people first learn to type, they usually improve quickly until they can type without looking at the keys. But after learning to "touch-type," they soon reach a plateau. No matter how much more they practice, they still don't type any faster. Even if they type every day for a living, all that practice doesn't continue to result in faster and faster typing.

In the 1960s, psychologists Paul Fitts and Michael Posner described the three stages of acquiring a new skill. The first phase is the "cognitive stage," wherein you consciously think about the task. The second phase is the "associative stage," wherein you improve your accuracy and efficiency and the task requires much less concentration. The third phase is the "autonomous stage," wherein you basically perform the skill automatically with barely any conscious effort at all.

This third stage is—of course—useful, because you can then pay more attention to *what* you are typing instead of how. All repetitive skills eventually reach the stage where you can free your mind to concentrate on other, more important things. This is true whether the skill is typing, driving, playing a sport... or reading.

But this final automatic stage can also be considered a plateau, because once you're good enough to no longer think about a skill, the skill no longer improves.

Some people, however, manage to surpass this plateau—continuing to improve and becoming true experts in their skill. Somehow these people find a way to avoid the plateau; this "way" is the process of *deliberate practice*.

These top achievers use a strategy to consciously stay away from that third, "good enough" stage. This strategy consists of three elements:

1. Focusing on <u>technique.</u>
2. Keeping attention on the <u>goal.</u>
3. Getting constant <u>feedback.</u>

By following this strategy, they force themselves to stay in the first cognitive stage.

The secret to reaching higher levels of any skill involves retaining conscious control while practicing and staying out of autopilot mode. This is why consciously concentrating on technique is so much more effective than simply putting in more hours of practice.

Maintaining conscious control of your practice works in a similar way to how conceptual reading works. Just as your comprehension and speed improves by staying consciously mindful of the *concepts* you are reading, your reading skill improves by staying consciously mindful of *how* you are reading.

All this additional concentration may seem challenging, but think about what you're doing—you are literally strengthening your brain. New discoveries about the neuroplasticity of the brain have demonstrated that the brain actually restructures itself to meet new cognitive demands. Training your brain to handle more information faster actually improves your brain's ability to assimilate information.

If your improvement slows down or plateaus, realize it's still all forward progress, and that the plateau is just something to pass through on the way to your goal.

Consistency

Practice is important, but if you want your mind to get the most return from your practice time, it helps to remember a few things about how the mind works. Memory storage is based on a web of neurons. Each new memory alters this web to leave what is called a memory trace. Each repetition of this memory further reinforces this trace, making it stronger and easier to access. These repetitions create long-lasting enhancements in the signal transmission capabilities between the neurons in this web. As a result, the more you practice a skill, the stronger your memory of that skill becomes.

Because repetition is such a powerful force in strengthening memories, consistency is an important component to learning any new skills. This is particularly true with reading, where you are trying to reprogram a very engrained habit which may be several years old. If you only work at it sporadically, your brain won't know you're serious and might try to ignore your attempts to change its way of thinking.

To maintain consistency, set a goal for yourself and plan the time period you will devote to practice; this will enable you to make use of the compounding effects of consistent practice.

You should also consider the length of time of each practice session and how far apart to space your practice. I discovered something unexpected when analyzing students' metadata on the associated online course (see online resources section). I found that speed improvement correlated more closely with words per day of practice, than with days per week. This seemed counter-intuitive, but by studying the millions of words read by thousands of students, I found that—on average—it turned out to actually be more productive to cram extra time into each practice than to practice more often. The results of this analysis showed a sixty-four percent correlation between reading improvement and minutes per day of practice, but no correlation (actually a negative 0.4% correlation) between successes and practice days per week.

On reflection, it seems this discovery might be in line with the latest science. According to Nassim Taleb's book *Antifragile*, the fastest growth of any type, whether physical or mental, occurs when an organism is prompted to overcompensate for significant stressors; it could be that longer practice sessions create this productive stress.

This is interesting because cramming more practice into fewer sessions is the opposite of how people are generally taught to study. I can't be sure this is what will work best for you, but these are the results I've found from other students, I'd at least like to offer the information for your consideration.

In the end, even though there are plenty of interesting theories and data on how to study, the best thing to do is to pay attention to what works for you. Pay attention to when and how you make the most progress, and then try to accommodate your own learning style.

Persistence

Homer: Hey, how come you never play your guitar anymore?

Bart: I'll tell ya the truth, Dad. I wasn't good at it right away, so I quit. I hope you're not mad.

Homer: [sweetly] Son, come here! Heh heh heh... [Bart sits on Homer's knee] Of course I'm not mad. If something's hard to do, then it's not worth doing! You just stick that guitar in the closet next to your short-wave radio, your karate outfit, and your unicycle, and we'll go inside and watch TV.

Obtaining a basic reading skill is a complex enough task on its own. Although achieving superior reading skills is even more difficult, the advantages are worth the effort. In the long run, *not* having good reading skills will end up costing you more than the effort needed to acquire them. Those without good reading skills are exiled to a land of ignorance—a boring wasteland, isolated from much of life's fascinations and excitement.

So how can you persist with the necessary effort to expand this skill? When you work on any goal, your motivation is bound to rise and fall over time and change with your moods; sometimes you will feel motivated, and sometimes you won't. But results don't come from motivation—they come from *action*.

Sometimes, when you don't feel like doing something that you know you should do, it helps if you fool yourself into taking action. Tell yourself that you are only going to practice for a few minutes, just enough to refresh your memory, and that if you feel like quitting after that, you'll allow yourself to go ahead and quit. However, you'll often find that once you overcome your initial desire to do nothing and instead get moving, the law of inertia works both ways; once a body (or a mind) is in motion, it tends to stay in motion. As a result, you may end up getting more done than you expected.

Patience

Although practice, consistency, and persistence are important ingredients for learning a skill, it can be a bitter mix without patience. Be patient with your progress. Allow time for your skills to develop. You may make great progress in the beginning when you first adopt this new perspective on reading, but don't get impatient when you get stuck. If you never got stuck, then you were probably pursuing a goal that was too easy.

When you do get stuck, slow down and concentrate more on the meaning of what you're reading. This change of speed can sometimes break you out of a rut, like rocking a car back and forth to get traction if you're stuck in a mud hole. This comprehension traction is important, and although it sounds like a contradiction, it means you will sometimes have to slow down to go faster.

However, if you simply try to push your speed, you will make a lot of comprehension errors, and these errors will end up slowing your overall speed. But if you back off just a bit and concentrate on accuracy—that is, concentrate on the concepts and ideas—you will reconnect to the information, and your reading will start to flow more smoothly, resulting in the desired speed increase.

You will also notice that your speed can increase and decrease, from one day to the next—or even one minute to the next. Sometimes this is due to the changing difficulty of the material, but it can also be due to your changing mental states. It's easy to slip out of "the zone" when you are distracted by other thoughts, and this makes it difficult to maintain a strong mental attachment to the material. Just be patient, put the book down, and attend to those other issues or distracting thoughts. Then, pick the book up again when you are ready for it.

Practice Exercise #5

With this exercise, be patient and concentrate on technique. If you are not seeing the ideas as you read, then you're wasting your time. Take a deep breath. Let it out slowly. Clear your mind and get ready to start the next reading practice.

When you're ready, begin reading the first thousand words of

Treasure Island by Robert Louis Stevenson

Treasure Island

Squire Trelawney, Dr. Livesey, and the rest of these gentlemen having asked me to write down the whole particulars about Treasure Island, from the beginning to the end, keeping nothing back but the bearings of the island, and that only because there is still treasure not yet lifted, I take up my pen in the year of grace 17 and go back to the time when my father kept the Admiral Benbow Inn and the brown old seaman with the saber cut first took up his lodging under our roof.

I remember him as if it were yesterday, as he came plodding to the inn door, his sea-chest following behind him in a hand-barrow—a tall, strong, heavy, nut-brown man, his tarry pigtail falling over the shoulder of his soiled blue coat, his hands ragged and scarred, with black, broken nails, and the saber cut across one cheek, a dirty, livid white. I remember him looking round the cover and whistling to himself as he did so, and then breaking out in that old sea-song that he sang so often afterwards:

"Fifteen men on the dead man's chest—Yo-ho-ho, and a bottle of rum!" in the high, old tottering voice that seemed to have been tuned and broken at the capstan bars. Then he rapped on the door with a bit of stick like a handspike that he carried, and when my father appeared, called roughly for a glass of rum. This, when it was brought to him, he drank slowly, like a connoisseur, lingering on the taste and still looking about him at the cliffs and up at our signboard.

"This is a handy cove," says he at length; "and a pleasantly situated grog-shop. Much company, mate?"

My father told him no, very little company, the more was the pity.

"Well, then," said he, "this is the berth for me. Here you, matey," he cried to the man who trundled the barrow; "bring up alongside and help up my chest. I'll stay here a bit," he continued. "I'm a plain man; rum and bacon and eggs is what I want, and that head up there for to watch ships off. What you might call me? You might call me captain. Oh, I see what you're at—there"; and he threw down three or four gold pieces on the threshold. "You can tell me when I've worked through that," says he, looking as fierce as a commander.

And indeed bad as his clothes were and coarsely as he spoke, he had none of the appearance of a man who sailed before the mast, but seemed like a mate or skipper accustomed to be obeyed or to strike. The man who came with the barrow told us the mail had set him down the morning before at the Royal George, that he had inquired what inns there were along the coast, and hearing ours well-spoken of, I suppose, and described as lonely, had chosen it from the others for his place of residence. And that was all we could learn of our guest.

He was a very silent man by custom. All day he hung round the cove or upon the cliffs with a brass telescope; all evening he sat in a corner of the parlor next to the fire and drank rum and water very strong. Mostly he would not speak when spoken to, only look up sudden and fierce and blow through his nose like a fog-horn; and we and the people who came about our house soon learned to let him be. Every day when he came back from his stroll he would ask if any seafaring men had gone by along the road. At first we thought it was the want of company of his own kind that made him ask this question, but at last we began to see he was desirous to avoid them. When a seaman did put up at the Admiral Benbow (as now and then some did, making by the coast road for Bristol) he would look in at him through the curtained door before he entered the parlor; and he was always sure to be as silent as a mouse when any such was present. For me, at least, there was no secret about the matter, for I was, in a way, a sharer in his alarms. He had taken me aside one day and promised me a silver four-penny on the first of every month if I would only keep my "weather-eye open for a seafaring man with one leg" and let him know the moment he appeared. Often enough when the first of the month came round and I applied to him for my wage, he would only blow through his nose at me and stare me down, but before the week was out he was sure to think better of it, bring me my four-penny piece, and repeat his orders to look out for "the seafaring man with one leg."

How that personage haunted my dreams, I need scarcely tell you. On stormy nights, when the wind shook the four corners of the house and the surf roared along the cove and up the cliffs, I would see him in a thousand forms, and with a thousand diabolical expressions. Now the leg would be cut off at the knee, now at the hip; now he was a monstrous kind of a creature who had never had but the one leg, and that in the middle of his body. To see him leap and run and pursue me over hedge and ditch was the worst of nightmares. And altogether I paid pretty dear for my monthly four-penny piece, in the shape of these abominable fancies.

But though I was so terrified by the idea of the seafaring man with one leg, I was far less afraid of the captain himself than anybody else who knew him. There were nights when he took a deal more rum and water than his head would carry; and then he would sometimes sit and sing his wicked, old, wild sea-songs, minding nobody; but sometimes he would call for glasses round and force all the trembling company to listen to his stories or bear a chorus to his singing. Often I have heard the house shaking with "Yo-ho-ho, and a bottle of rum," all the neighbors joining in for dear life, with the fear of death upon them, and...

Chapter 6: Ancient History

Reading is everywhere we look. It is such a prevalent part of our lives that it's difficult to imagine a world without it. But even the most basic form of written text didn't appear until about five thousand years ago, and it wasn't until only five hundred years ago that reading became common among the general population.

A short discussion of the history of reading will make it easier to understand the skill that we seek to improve. Seeing reading in the context of where it came from, and how it got to where it is now, will also demonstrate why the way we read now, is not necessarily the final stage in our development of this amazing ability.

Our species has been sending each other messages for one hundred fifty thousand years, but *written* messages are a much more recent innovation.

It's a shame that children aren't told the story of reading and instead are left with the erroneous impression that reading has somehow always existed. Learning to read is more interesting when you realize that this is a new technology, and that only a few centuries ago it was even considered magic.

Reading developed through a process of trial and error and was created in stages. Each of these stages was a modification to suit the particular needs of the people at that time.

Reading and writing aren't fixed skills that have been passed down to us intact—each generation has added its own improvements as it saw fit. Reading has always been a dynamic skill; therefore, there is no reason to believe its development ended when it was handed down to us. People invented reading, and people are free to continue improving it for as long as they want.

Alphabet

The first written language was developed by the Sumerians and the Egyptians about fifty-four hundred years ago. They created it as a way to keep track of agricultural trading, and this idea of using symbols for record keeping is what eventually grew into writing as we know it today.

The Sumerians developed a method of writing using cuneiforms, symbols pressed into clay tablets.

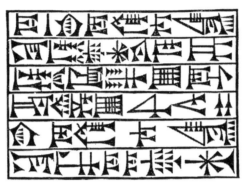

The Egyptians developed a method of using hieroglyphics and pictograms written with charcoal on papyrus.

Since it was faster and easier to draw pictograms on papyrus than to carve cuneiforms in clay, the Egyptians began expanding their pictograms to also represent the sounds of consonants. In this way, besides keeping track of items being traded, they were also able to record names and events.

This recording of consonants was a major turning point in human history; for the first time, the sounds of actual speech could be saved. With the introduction of consonants, simple record keeping evolved into actual writing, and human thought could now be communicated over time and distance.

The word "hieroglyph" is Greek for *sacred writing*. It's easy to understand why it was considered sacred when you imagine what a magical experience reading must have been. What must people have thought when they discovered that just by looking at these hieroglyphs, they could hear voices in their heads? Writing must have seemed almost alive to them.

Around thirty-eight hundred years ago, the Phoenicians, a people of traders and sailors, needed a faster and simpler system than those currently available to them. Cuneiform and hieroglyphic writings were comprised of hundreds of symbols and were so complex that they were only reserved for a small caste of specialists. The Phoenicians created a system of representing sounds (phonics) by adapting a small set of these hieroglyphic symbols. Because there were fewer symbols, this new Phoenician alphabet was easy to learn and simple to use.

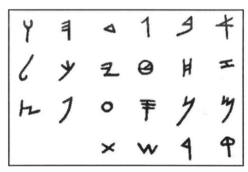

The Phoenician alphabet, however, was only composed of consonants, so pictures were occasionally added to remove ambiguities. To clarify this even further, the Greeks modified the Phoenician alphabet by adding vowels.

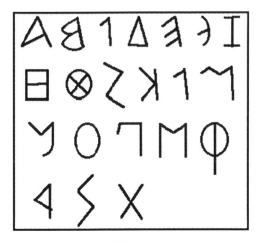

This alphabet was then adapted by the Romans about twenty-seven hundred years ago to form the Latin alphabet. Then Latin was adapted by the English around sixteen hundred years ago to form the Old English alphabet. The Old English alphabet continued to be modified until around two hundred years ago when we arrived at the English alphabet used today.

Spaces and Punctuation

Originally there was no punctuation. It wasn't until about twenty-two hundred years ago that the most basic punctuation marks were invented by Aristophanes of Byzantium, the director of the Library of Alexandria. This punctuation consisted of a single dot either at the bottom, middle, or top of the line to let readers know how long to pause between sentences.

Even spaces had to be invented. Until they were, words ran together in an unending stream of capital letters known as *scriptio continua*. ASYOUCANSEEITISNOTVERYEASYTOREADLIKETHIS

About thirteen hundred years ago, Irish monks began using spaces to separate words in Latin and, for the first time ever, we had individual words.

Before spaces, text functioned more like musical notes, and a person reading a scroll was more like a player piano, translating the scroll into sounds. In fact, well into the Middle Ages, reading was an activity generally carried out aloud; text was usually spoken as a kind of performance. The performers would practice and repeat their performances, and the text only had to serve as a reminder.

But by adding spaces and punctuation, text became more meaningful as ideas instead of just sounds; and rather than replicating speech, some readers began to read completely in their heads—especially in the monastery libraries where they had to be very quiet.

Over time, further improvements were added to make written language easier to read. By around twelve hundred years ago, spacing had become popular and the catalog of punctuation marks had grown richer. By this time, the page provided enough information for silent reading finally to become common.

Printing Press

After the printing press appeared in the late 1400s, the popularity of reading absolutely exploded. The printing press was like the World Wide Web of the day; suddenly, the world was full of information that had never been available before. As more and more information became available, more and more people began to read.

Although many could read silently, most reading was still considered simply a form of entertainment, and—just like television entertainment today—was best enjoyed when shared. People would read to each other, and public reading performances were a common form of entertainment. The wealthy even hired people to read to them at home—the audio book of the time.

But as the amount of reading material available continued to grow, and the time available for reading remained relatively fixed, the ability to read faster became increasingly desirable.

However since reading was considered a verbal performance, how would it be possible to read faster than you could speak? Even if you only thought the words internally, how could you think them faster without it sounding like gibberish? The answer is to concentrate on the whole ideas being expressed rather than the sounds of the spoken words. This means that it is not enough to just read silently or even to avoid sub-vocalizing, but to concentrate on imagining *what* is being communicated instead of the *words* used to communicate it.

Practice Exercise #6

As you read the next practice exercise, make sure to see each phrase as a complete, meaningful piece of information. Just as spaces divide letters into distinct words, phrases divide words into complete and independent ideas. Concentrate on these ideas rather than the words. You are not performing the text; you are absorbing ideas.

When you're ready, begin reading the first thousand words of

The Wonderful Wizard of Oz by L. Frank Baum

The Wonderful Wizard of Oz

Dorothy lived in the midst of the great Kansas prairies, with Uncle Henry, who was a farmer, and Aunt Em, who was the farmer's wife. Their house was small, for the lumber to build it had to be carried by wagon many miles. There were four walls, a floor and a roof, which made one room; and this room contained a rusty looking cook-stove, a cupboard for the dishes, a table, three or four chairs, and the beds. Uncle Henry and Aunt Em had a big bed in one corner, and Dorothy a little bed in another corner. There was no garret at all, and no cellar— except a small hole dug in the ground, called a cyclone cellar, where the family could go in case one of those great whirlwinds arose, mighty enough to crush any building in its path. It was reached by a trap door in the middle of the floor, from which a ladder led down into the small, dark hole.

When Dorothy stood in the doorway and looked around, she could see nothing but the great gray prairie on every side. Not a tree nor a house broke the broad sweep of flat country that reached to the edge of the sky in all directions. The sun had baked the plowed land into a gray mass, with little cracks running through it. Even the grass was not green, for the sun had burned the tops of the long blades until they were the same gray color to be seen everywhere. Once the house had been painted, but the sun blistered the paint and the rains washed it away, and now the house was as dull and gray as everything else.

When Aunt Em came there to live she was a young, pretty wife. The sun and wind had changed her, too. They had taken the sparkle from her eyes and left them a sober gray; they had taken the red from her cheeks and lips, and they were gray also. She was thin and gaunt, and never smiled now. When Dorothy, who was an orphan, first came to her, Aunt Em had been so startled by the child's laughter that she would scream and press her hand upon her heart whenever Dorothy's merry voice reached her ears; and she still looked at the little girl with wonder that she could find anything to laugh at.

Uncle Henry never laughed. He worked hard from morning till night and did not know what joy was. He was gray also, from his long beard to his rough boots, and he looked stern and solemn, and rarely spoke.

It was Toto that made Dorothy laugh, and saved her from growing as gray as her other surroundings. Toto was not gray; he was a little black dog, with long silky hair and small black eyes that twinkled merrily on either side of his funny, wee nose. Toto played all day long, and Dorothy played with him, and loved him dearly.

Today, however, they were not playing. Uncle Henry sat upon the doorstep and looked anxiously at the sky, which was even grayer than usual. Dorothy stood in the door with Toto in her arms, and looked at the sky too. Aunt Em was washing the dishes.

From the far north they heard a low wail of the wind, and Uncle Henry and Dorothy could see where the long grass bowed in waves before the coming storm. There now came a sharp whistling in the air from the south, and as they turned their eyes that way they saw ripples in the grass coming from that direction also.

Suddenly Uncle Henry stood up.

"There's a cyclone coming, Em," he called to his wife. "I'll go look after the stock." Then he ran toward the sheds where the cows and horses were kept.

Aunt Em dropped her work and came to the door. One glance told her of the danger close at hand.

"Quick, Dorothy!" she screamed. "Run for the cellar!"

Toto jumped out of Dorothy's arms and hid under the bed, and the girl started to get him. Aunt Em, badly frightened, threw open the trap door in the floor and climbed down the ladder into the small, dark hole. Dorothy caught Toto at last and started to follow her aunt. When she was halfway across the room there came a great shriek from the wind, and the house shook so hard that she lost her footing and sat down suddenly upon the floor.

Then a strange thing happened.

The house whirled around two or three times and rose slowly through the air. Dorothy felt as if she were going up in a balloon.

The north and south winds met where the house stood, and made it the exact center of the cyclone. In the middle of a cyclone the air is generally still, but the great pressure of the wind on every side of the house raised it up higher and higher, until it was at the very top of the cyclone; and there it remained and was carried miles and miles away as easily as you could carry a feather.

It was very dark, and the wind howled horribly around her, but Dorothy found she was riding quite easily. After the first few whirls around, and one other time when the house tipped badly, she felt as if she were being rocked gently, like a baby in a cradle.

Toto did not like it. He ran about the room, now here, now there, barking loudly; but Dorothy sat quite still on the floor and waited to see what would happen.

Once Toto got too near the open trap door, and fell in; and at first the little girl thought she had lost him. But soon she saw one of his ears sticking up through the hole, for the strong pressure of the air was keeping him up so that he could not fall. She crept to the hole, caught Toto by the ear, and dragged him into the room again, afterward closing the trap door so that no more accidents could happen.

Hour after hour passed away, and slowly Dorothy got over her fright; but she felt quite lonely, and the wind shrieked so loudly all about her that she nearly became deaf. At first she had wondered if she would be...

Chapter 7: Modern History

So, what is "speed reading," and where did the idea of speed reading come from? There are almost as many definitions of what speed reading is as there are courses and books on the subject, and the history of speed reading is clouded with many myths and misconceptions. However, knowing the real story of speed reading will further clarify the process and goal of real reading improvement.

Speed Reading

Origins

The speed of normal spoken English is about one hundred fifty words per minute. The way to read faster than you speak is to do away with this speech and replace it with ideas. Instead of internally verbalizing the words, why not simply think the thoughts? This would allow more than one word at a time to be read, and it would omit the necessity of internal verbalizing, because once the idea was understood, the reading job would be done.

The concept of reading groups of words at a time has been around since 1879, when a French ophthalmologist, Louis Émile Javal, developed a method of photographically recording people's eye movements while they read. Until then, everyone simply "knew" the eyes had to look at each letter in every word.

The interesting thing is, readers don't move their eyes in a smooth flow, but in small jerking motions called fixations. Javal's photographs recorded these fixations and revealed that while poor readers perceived just one word—or perhaps only a part of a word—at a time, excellent readers took in entire groups of words with each eye fixation. After this discovery, instructors began to encourage students to "widen their eye spans" and see as many words as they could at each fixation.

The invention of the tachistoscope—a machine designed to flash a series of images very rapidly, sometimes allowing them to appear on the screen for only 1/100th of a second, in order to create subliminal imprinting in the mind—seemed to create an advancement in teaching students to see more words at a time. This technology, invented by psychologist Dr. Samuel Renshaw, was originally used to train World War II naval soldiers to rapidly recognize different aircraft and ships.

In 1946, Dr. Renshaw patented the tachistoscope projector and began directing research at Ohio State University to use the machine to teach speed reading.

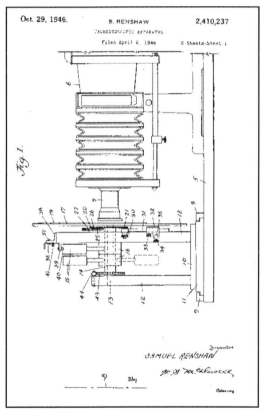

With regular training on the machine, most people were able to increase their reading speeds from an average of two hundred words per minute to an average of four hundred per minute—the difference between the junior high school student and the post-graduate. However, most students reported that shortly after their course finished, their reading speeds once again sank to their previous levels.

Only recently have experts realized that the normal range of reading ability is roughly two hundred to four hundred words per minute, and that most people operate at the lower end of this range. The increased reading abilities observed during the tachistoscopic courses actually had little to do with the training; they were mostly due to the students being highly motivated over a period of weeks and thus being able to reach the top of their normal range.

Although it was gradually recognized that the tachistoscopic method did not provide any lasting positive results, this approach was still offered as a part of the basic training kit of most speed reading courses for many years. After all, they had to offer something, and a machine like this made a good first impression on students.

Recent History

Before the 1920s, reading instruction stressed "accurate *oral* reading." The good reader was one who could "read *aloud* with *expression* and *fluency*."

But then experimenters at the University of Chicago found that students could read faster silently than they could orally, and they could do it with better comprehension and retention. Research on eye movement during this time also found that a reader could read faster if he made fewer fixations per line of text.

However, further research showed that eye movement could not be consciously controlled. Most authorities concluded that the only way to improve reading would be to improve the reader's ability to *perceive* and *interpret* the material. Therefore, by the 1950s most teachers and colleges were already skeptical of any courses labeled "speed reading."

But then in 1959, a woman named Evelyn Nielsen Wood set up a course in Wilmington, Delaware called Reading Dynamics. Wood's method started with what she called "push-up" drills, wherein students would read for one minute and then re-read, trying to cover more material each time. The course also concentrated on exercises meant to widen the eye span in order to see more words at a time. To eliminate subvocalizing, students were encouraged to push their speeds faster than they could vocalize.

Even though these courses concentrated on pushing your speed, the basic theory behind Wood's exercises was that students should concentrate on reading thoughts instead of words. She described it like this: *"The reader becomes part of the story. Since the method relies upon the total idea of the thought rather than the individual words, there is no feeling of hurry or fast motion of speeded reading. The words go in fast, but they go in only to make the complete picture."*

Evelyn Wood considered her work an important crusade—one that would improve student reading skills across the country. In the fall of 1960, she set out to change the world, opening twenty-five instruction centers around the United States.

Sadly though, Wood was bankrupt by the following September. She had opened all twenty-five centers within one month, and although Wood had a zealous commitment towards her schools, she unfortunately did not have any real business or advertising experience.

She sold her business to George Webster, who promptly fired the original staff and modified the course and the marketing. He ran a simply worded full-page ad in the newspaper, offering a money-back guarantee if a student didn't at least triple their "reading index." Suddenly, Reading Dynamics became a huge success, and Wood was hired to make public appearances and open new schools.

The advertised guarantee was a very effective marketing strategy, but unfortunately for students, the guarantee wasn't really that easy to qualify for.

First, the promise was only to improve the student's so-called "reading index." This index was calculated by multiplying the words-per-minute speed by the comprehension score. It was actually difficult *not* to improve this index since the final reading exercise was always so much easier than the first. The final comprehension test was so easy that students could score quite high without even reading the exercise.

Second, students had to complete the entire course before qualifying for the refund, and most unsatisfied customers just dropped out, choosing to lose their money rather than more of their time.

In the end, few students actually made the incredible progress that was promised. Over the next twenty years the public became more and more skeptical, and the "speed reading" industry was unable to refute this skepticism with enough student success stories.

This skepticism is unfortunate because there are always ways to improve any skill. But because of the outlandish promises made by many of these courses, people felt cheated and then ridiculed all speed reading courses to avoid looking foolish enough to fall for such ridiculous promises. As comedian Woody Allen described it, "I took a speed reading course and read *War and Peace* in twenty minutes... It involves Russia."

Progress

Although the past century was littered with many courses using all kinds of incredible exercises and making even more incredible claims, at least the past hundred years saw a huge increase in the number of people who actually *could* read.

In the century before that, a lot fewer people could read—and most who did, only read aloud, and only for entertainment. But even as a form of entertainment, reading was probably as fascinating to the people of that time as any of our entertainment is to us today. It's interesting when you realize that before there was radio or TV, most people never even heard what people in other places sounded like. In fact, this is why many books of the 1800s—*Tom Sawyer* is a good example—are so full of colloquialisms and strangely spelled words. These books were written this way to reproduce the way people *sounded.*

Throughout the twentieth century, reading instruction became much more widely available than in previous eras; however, it was still primarily aimed at reading sounds, not ideas.

Future Reading

Reading has made great progress over the centuries, but that doesn't mean the progress has to stop now. With the recent erosion in reading skills, there is now even greater room for improvement. Today half the people read below two hundred words per minute, the vast majority of high school graduates aren't ready for college, and SAT reading scores have plummeted to their lowest level in four decades. The best path out of this this problem is through improved reading skills. The good news is that this is something people can do on their own.

Due to the massive and rapidly growing amount of information available since the advent of computers, the internet, and e-books, reading skills are becoming ever more important. Information is no longer expensive or difficult to access, and this means that regardless of the issues we may have with our current educational systems, we seem to be entering a new era of do-it-yourself education—and the only entrance exam or tuition required is the ability to read.

In order to read more, reading needs to evolve beyond text as sound to text as meaning. This is the same goal Evelyn Wood suggested when she said we needed to *rely more upon the total idea of thought rather than the individual words.*"

But now there is an important difference: the order. Comprehension must come first, *before* speed. Wood's method was basically an improvement on the old tachistoscopes—it still focused on pushing speed and merely hoped for improved comprehension as a result. The reverse, however, is the better way to read faster. Faster reading won't lead to faster comprehension, but faster comprehension will naturally lead to faster reading.

There have been many disagreements over methods to teach reading, but when people think of controversies in reading education, they usually only consider disagreements about word recognition training—such as the long-standing argument between phonics and sight learning. Both of these methods only teach how to match text with words, but regardless of which method is used to recognize words, word recognition is really only the first step of reading.

To be an effective reader, you need to be able to rapidly and accurately process the thoughts behind the words. The thoughts are what the author wanted to communicate; the words were used only as a vehicle to communicate them.

The history of writing has gone from simple record-keeping, to sound recording, and then to idea recording. Reading now has to catch up and advance from sound playback to *idea* playback. To handle the more extensive and sophisticated information today, we'll need to trade in listening to that old-time radio and switch over to watching a new HD flat screen.

In other words, this is not your parents' reading. If reading and writing has changed so much in the past, it would be incredibly vain of us to think that we, today, were the intended final receivers of this skill. Likewise, it would be shameful to think we were the first who could not improve it.

Practice Exercise #7

Remember, if you find yourself slipping into old reading habits as you practice, just stop a moment and then continue by concentrating more on meaning. As you continue, go as slowly as you need to until you can really get a grasp on the information. Take your time; you're creating something new. This whole human ability to read may still be on the ground floor, and you are experimenting with using other parts of your brain to discover a better way of extracting meaning from text.

And if it seems sometimes like you're not quite sure how to conceptualize the ideas you are reading, and you feel like you're not quite getting it, imagine how earlier readers felt when they first tried reading in their heads. That probably felt pretty strange too, and I'm sure they often felt impelled to start reading aloud again as they were used to doing. No reading advancements would have occurred if people weren't willing to try something new, so read with an open mind, so you too can be part of this advancement.

Just as with your previous six exercises, see each word-group in a single glance, imagine the meaning of each phrase, concentrate on pushing your comprehension instead of your speed, and be patient and focus on the ideas.

When you're ready, begin reading the first thousand words of

The Adventures of Tom Sawyer by **Mark Twain**

The Adventures of Tom Sawyer

"TOM!"

No answer.

"TOM!"

No answer.

"What's gone with that boy, I wonder? You TOM!"

No answer.

The old lady pulled her spectacles down and looked over them about the room; then she put them up and looked out under them. She seldom or never looked THROUGH them for so small a thing as a boy; they were her state pair, the pride of her heart, and were built for "style," not service—she could have seen through a pair of stove-lids just as well. She looked perplexed for a moment, and then said, not fiercely, but still loud enough for the furniture to hear:

"Well, I lay if I get hold of you I'll—"

She did not finish, for by this time she was bending down and punching under the bed with the broom, and so she needed breath to punctuate the punches with. She resurrected nothing but the cat.

"I never did see the beat of that boy!"

She went to the open door and stood in it and looked out among the tomato vines and "jimpson" weeds that constituted the garden. No Tom. So she lifted up her voice at an angle calculated for distance and shouted:

"Y-o-u-u TOM!"

There was a slight noise behind her and she turned just in time to seize a small boy by the slack of his roundabout and arrest his flight.

"There! I might 'a' thought of that closet. What you been doing in there?"

"Nothing."

"Nothing! Look at your hands. And look at your mouth. What IS that truck?"

"I don't know, Aunt."

"Well, I know. It's jam—that's what it is. Forty times I've said if you didn't let that jam alone I'd skin you. Hand me that switch."

The switch hovered in the air—the peril was desperate—

"My! Look behind you, Aunt!"

The old lady whirled round, and snatched her skirts out of danger. The lad fled on the instant, scrambled up the high board-fence, and disappeared over it.

His Aunt Polly stood surprised a moment, and then broke into a gentle laugh.

"Hang the boy, can't I never learn anything? Ain't he played me tricks enough like that for me to be looking out for him by this time? But old fools is the biggest fools there is. Can't learn an old dog new tricks, as the saying is. But my goodness, he never plays them alike, two days, and how is a body to know what's coming? He 'pears to know just how long he can torment me before I get my dander up, and he knows if he can make out to put me off for a minute or make me laugh, it's all down again and I can't hit him a lick. I ain't doing my duty by that boy, and that's the Lord's truth, goodness knows. Spare the rod and spile the child, as the Good Book says. I'm a laying up sin and suffering for us both, I know. He's full of the Old Scratch, but laws-a-me! He's my own dead sister's boy, poor thing, and I ain't got the heart to lash him, somehow. Every time I let him off, my conscience does hurt me so, and every time I hit him my old heart most breaks. Well-a-well, man that is born of woman is of few days and full of trouble, as the Scripture says, and I reckon it's so. He'll play hookey this afternoon, and I'll just be obleeged to make him work, tomorrow, to punish him. It's mighty hard to make him work Saturdays, when all the boys is having holiday, but he hates work more than he hates anything else, and I've GOT to do some of my duty by him, or I'll be the ruination of the child."

Tom did play hookey, and he had a very good time. He got back home barely in season to help Jim, the small colored boy, saw next-day's wood and split the kindlings before supper—at least he was there in time to tell his adventures to Jim while Jim did three-fourths of the work. Tom's younger brother (or rather half-brother) Sid was already through with his part of the work (picking up chips), for he was a quiet boy, and had no adventurous, troublesome ways.

While Tom was eating his supper, and stealing sugar as opportunity offered, Aunt Polly asked him questions that were full of guile, and very deep—for she wanted to trap him into damaging revealments. Like many other simple-hearted souls, it was her pet vanity to believe she was endowed with a talent for dark and mysterious diplomacy, and she loved to contemplate her most transparent devices as marvels of low cunning. Said she:

"Tom, it was middling warm in school, warn't it?"

"Yes'm."

"Powerful warm, warn't it?"

"Yes'm."

"Didn't you want to go in a-swimming, Tom?"

A bit of a scare shot through Tom—a touch of uncomfortable suspicion. He searched Aunt Polly's face, but it told him nothing. So he said:

"No'm—well, not very much."

The old lady reached out her hand and felt Tom's shirt, and said:

"But you ain't too warm now, though." And it flattered her to reflect that she had discovered that the shirt was dry without anybody knowing that that was what she had in her mind. But in spite of her, Tom knew where the wind lay, now. So he forestalled what might be the next move:

"Some of us pumped on our heads—mine's damp yet. See?"

Aunt Polly was vexed to think she had overlooked that bit of circumstantial evidence, and missed a trick. Then she had a new inspiration:

"Tom, you didn't have to undo your shirt collar where I sewed it, to pump on your head, did you? Unbutton your jacket!"

The trouble vanished out of Tom's face. He opened his jacket. His shirt collar was securely sewed.

"Bother! Well, go 'long with you. I'd made sure you'd played hookey and been a-swimming. But I forgive ye, Tom. I reckon you're a kind of a singed cat, as the saying is—better'n you look. THIS time."

She was half sorry her sagacity had miscarried, and half glad that Tom had stumbled into obedient conduct for once.

But Sidney said:

"Well, now...

Chapter 8: Texting the Brain

Thinking about how you are reading, *while* you are reading, can seem counterproductive because the extra effort required would obviously distract you from your comprehension. You can really only think of one thing at a time, so thinking about what your brain is doing would interfere with thinking about what you are reading.

But having an overall concept of how the brain reads will help you practice more effectively. An overview of what your brain is doing and what you are trying to change, will help you stay on the right track and stay focused on the techniques that will get your right brain involved in your reading.

It's not necessary to stay consciously aware of this process while you read, but removing some of the mystery may leave you with a general lay of the land, to make it easier to know where you are going and make your progress more straightforward.

Mechanics

In basic terms, text is a communication device and the reader's mind is a receiver. Just like a text message sent from one smart phone to another, printed words are sent from the page to your brain. In both cases, a signal is being sent, received, and decoded.

How does the brain actually accomplish this task? How can you know someone's thoughts simply by looking at squiggles on a page? It seems like some kind of magic that these printed marks are actually speaking to your brain. How is this possible? Text enters the eyes like any other image, but how do images of text turn into thoughts? Where and how does real reading take place?

This is not a course on neurolinguistics—and anyone who is an expert in the field is invited to clarify any essential discrepancies—but some basic concepts will be useful, so here are a few simple glimpses under the hood to help conceptualize what is involved.

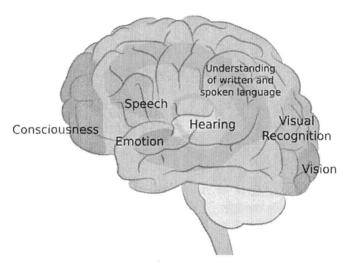

Like all mental tasks, reading uses a network of modules and systems, each relying on its own network of neurons. Many areas of the brain work together simultaneously, and while the complete process is not even entirely understood yet, a general awareness of how reading is accomplished can give you a deeper respect for the amazing complexity involved, as well as an appreciation of how and why reading with the right brain boosts your reading effectiveness.

One network of neurons, which many people may not think of as an actual part of the brain, is the eye. Reading starts with light entering the eye. And even though the whole eye is filled with light, only the fovea—a portion of the retina which occupies about fifteen degrees of the visual field—is used for reading.

Signals from the fovea are transferred to the occipital lobe at the back of the brain, where the light signals are recognized as shapes. From this point on, these shapes are converted into words in a step-by-step process along a path through the left side of the brain.

The recognized shapes are passed from the occipital lobe to the visual recognition area, where shapes are recognized as letters, then passed further forward to the Wernicke's area. This is the area which understands both written or spoken language. This area recognizes the groups of letters as words. From here, the information branches off in several more directions.

The words are sent farther forward to the hearing area in the auditory cortex, where they can be subvocalized, plus along a separate path to Broca's area, where speech production is controlled for saying words aloud.

At the same time the words are also sent down into the center of the brain to the amygdala, where the emotional content is determined. It may not seem like emotions would affect reading, but memories are more likely to stick if they are combined with emotion. This is one reason that having an interest in a subject makes it easier to remember; being interested in something activates the powerful emotion of pleasure.

But there's much more to reading than just recognizing words. Real meaning only comes from the way the words are *combined*, and in that one fact lies the real secret to reading faster...

Think Fast

Quick! Memorize the following letters:

U P S I R S F B I J F K N A S A N A T O

Not done yet? Fine. Give up then, because it really does take too long.

But let's make it easier by grouping the same string of letters like this:

UPSI RSFB IJF KNA SAN ATO

Easier, right? Just six little "words" to remember. Nope. Still too hard and still takes too much time.

Well, what if we group the letters like this:

UPS IRS FBI JFK NASA NATO

Wow, what a difference! The letters still make up six words, but these words are so much easier to remember than the previous ones. They're made up of the same letters, in the same order, and in the same number of "words," but only the grouping is different. Now they're grouped into phrases, with each phrase representing a meaningful chunk of information.

This is the key to moving more information through your brain faster: parceling the information into larger packages. Reading and remembering takes a lot of thinking, and thinking takes time. You can't really make those neurons fire any faster than they are capable; as smart as they are, they still have certain physical limits.

I don't mean that neurons are slow, but it just takes an awful lot of firing on their part to accomplish all the work they have to do as they sort and store information. When they're resting, neurons fire about twenty-five times per second. When they're active, that speed increases to around four hundred times per second. And when they're concentrating really hard on something, they max out at about one thousand firings per second. So yes, you *can* think faster, but there is still a maximum speed limit.

There are other limits, too. Besides processing speed, our conscious minds can only hold about seven pieces of information at a time; and at normal reading speeds, these pieces only have about half a second before the next piece comes through.

But fortunately there is a clever way to bypass both of these limitations. In fact, this solution is a special talent that, in comparison to all other creatures, puts humans at the head of the pack in the thinking department. Although humans aren't well known for physical strength, speed, or any other particularly powerful physical abilities, they do excel at *consciousness*. Human consciousness gives rise to an amazing ability to handle novel and complex information, which allows humans to invent new solutions to problems and to make accurate predictions about the future.

This consciousness is not located throughout the whole brain, but resides primarily in the prefrontal cortex. This is where you pay attention. This is where the real "you" lives.

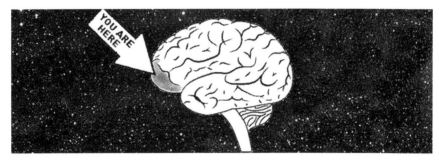

This prefrontal cortex is the erasable whiteboard of the brain; here, information is scribbled temporarily while the consciousness decides what to do with it. Information constantly and rapidly flows into this area from the senses and is quickly organized, filtered, and chunked together into larger ideas. And it has to accomplish all this even though it only has room to hold about seven pieces of information at a time.

But the conscious mind uses a clever trick to keep up with all this information. Although it is limited to handling only about seven items at a time, each of these items can be immensely complex. Each of these seven items can be piled high with information, similar to the way we pile food on our plates at an all-you-can-eat buffet. Chunking of information into larger more complex ideas makes the most of each conceptual idea before it is sent on to memory.

The key to this process of filtering and combining information is the brain's fascination with *patterns* and *hidden structures*. These patterns allow ideas and concepts to be assembled into massively complex pyramids of information where each thought is attached to many layers of underlying meaning and associations.

This hunger for patterns is unstoppable. We can't help seeing patterns in everything. The result is more than just faster thinking, but also richer experiences. By filtering and combining information into larger patterns, we create the complex context of our consciousness. We don't just see, learn, and remember information—we *understand* it conceptually. To conceptualize information is to become truly aware of it, and what it means to us.

The process of chunking information into conceptual patterns is not just a neat trick for thinking and reading faster—the more we chunk information into concepts, the more truly conscious we become.

Reading Evolution

As amazing as the human mind is, it wasn't specifically designed for the modern world. Our minds evolved and developed over a period of time continually adapting to our changing needs.

So just like language, our minds are just what we ended up with. Our brains weren't designed with reading in mind. Our early hominid ancestors needed to know things like where food and resources were, the route home, and which plants were edible or poisonous.

To recognize these types of things, they had to be very good at visual imagery, but they didn't have to remember things like lists of facts, or names, dates, and numbers. They also didn't need to spend much time thinking about abstract ideas—the kinds with no visual associations.

Since reading was only developed a few thousand years ago, it certainly hasn't given our brains enough time for any physical adaptation. In essence, we are still reading with prehistoric brains, yet somehow there are fixed circuitries of the human brain that seem perfectly attuned to recognizing the printed word.

What appears to have happened is that somehow humans have very effectively reassigned portions of their brains to this new task. In other words, reading looks to be just a patch onto an existing, more primitive brain. But even though this reassignment of brain areas is just a makeshift adaptation, our reading skills have continued on a constant path of improvement and sophistication. They have progressed from recognizing cave pictures to rapidly consuming vast amounts of data from a continuous flow of complex information.

This has been an incredible mental restructuring. A caveman has learned to read. If the brain developed this amazing skill in such a short time, then once again, it makes one wonder how we could imagine that our current reading skill is the "finished" product.

Practice Exercise #8

For the next reading exercise, imagine how your inner caveman brain is going to understand this. This guy has been around way longer than those shiny, brand new reading skills—and he prefers to think in pictures! So make sure to give him something that will keep his attention by forming visual images that will be interesting to the whole brain.

One thing you could try if you are having difficulty thinking in pictures as you read is doodling the phrases. To prompt your mind to think visually, try this exercise. Get a sheet of paper and make very quick sketches of what each phrase means to you. These can be absolutely simplistic and maybe only meaningful to you. Don't take a lot of time, just jot down whatever comes to mind, be it an actual pictorial view, a metaphorical view, or a symbolic view. These aren't pieces of art and should be created as quickly as possible—just simple stick figures will do. Think of it as speed *Pictionary*.

Don't be concerned at all about what your doodles look like; just as our internal singing voice is often better than what comes out of our mouths, our right brains will internally take care of the real artwork much better than we can draw. The point is only to give you some practice in seeing ideas as images and concepts, which can help wake up the visual right brain.

When you're ready, begin reading the first thousand words of

The Strange Case of Dr. Jekyll and Mr. Hyde
by Robert Louis Stevenson

The Strange Case of Dr. Jekyll and Mr. Hyde

Mr. Utterson the lawyer was a man of a rugged countenance, that was never lighted by a smile; cold, scanty and embarrassed in discourse; backward in sentiment; lean, long, dusty, dreary, and yet somehow lovable. At friendly meetings, and when the wine was to his taste, something eminently human beaconed from his eye; something indeed which never found its way into his talk, but which spoke not only in these silent symbols of the after-dinner face, but more often and loudly in the acts of his life. He was austere with himself; drank gin when he was alone, to mortify a taste for vintages; and though he enjoyed the theatre, had not crossed the doors of one for twenty years. But he had an approved tolerance for others; sometimes wondering, almost with envy, at the high pressure of spirits involved in their misdeeds; and in any extremity inclined to help rather than to reprove.

"I incline to Cain's heresy," he used to say quaintly: "I let my brother go to the devil in his own way." In this character, it was frequently his fortune to be the last reputable acquaintance and the last good influence in the lives of down-going men. And to such as these, so long as they came about his chambers, he never marked a shade of change in his demeanor.

No doubt the feat was easy to Mr. Utterson; for he was undemonstrative at the best, and even his friendship seemed to be founded in a similar catholicity of good-nature. It is the mark of a modest man to accept his friendly circle ready-made from the hands of opportunity; and that was the lawyer's way. His friends were those of his own blood or those whom he had known the longest; his affections, like ivy, were the growth of time, they implied no aptness in the object. Hence, no doubt, the bond that united him to Mr. Richard Enfield, his distant kinsman, the well-known man about town. It was a nut to crack for many, what these two could see in each other, or what subject they could find in common. It was reported by those who encountered them in their Sunday walks, that they said nothing, looked singularly dull, and would hail with obvious relief the appearance of a friend. For all that, the two men put the greatest store by these excursions, counted them the chief jewel of each week, and not only set aside occasions of pleasure, but even resisted the calls of business, that they might enjoy them uninterrupted.

It chanced on one of these rambles that their way led them down a by-street in a busy quarter of London. The street was small and what is called quiet, but it drove a thriving trade on the week-days. The inhabitants were all doing well, it seemed, and all emulously hoping to do better still, and laying out the surplus of their gains in coquetry; so that the shop fronts stood along that thoroughfare with an air of invitation, like rows of smiling saleswomen. Even on Sunday, when it veiled its more florid charms and lay comparatively empty of passage, the street shone out in contrast to its dingy neighborhood, like a fire in a forest; and with its freshly painted shutters, well-polished brasses, and general cleanliness and gaiety of note, instantly caught and pleased the eye of the passenger.

Two doors from one corner, on the left hand going east, the line was broken by the entry of a court; and just at that point, a certain sinister block of building thrust forward its gable on the street. It was two stories high; showed no window, nothing but a door on the lower story and a blind forehead of discolored wall on the upper; and bore in every feature, the marks of prolonged and sordid negligence. The door, which was equipped with neither bell nor knocker, was blistered and distained. Tramps slouched into the recess and struck matches on the panels; children kept shop upon the steps; the schoolboy had tried his knife on the moldings; and for close on a generation, no one had appeared to drive away these random visitors or to repair their ravages.

Mr. Enfield and the lawyer were on the other side of the by-street; but when they came abreast of the entry, the former lifted up his cane and pointed.

"Did you ever remark that door?" he asked; and when his companion had replied in the affirmative, "It is connected in my mind," added he, "with a very odd story."

"Indeed?" said Mr. Utterson, with a slight change of voice, "and what was that?"

"Well, it was this way," returned Mr. Enfield: "I was coming home from some place at the end of the world, about three o'clock of a black winter morning, and my way lay through a part of town where there was literally nothing to be seen but lamps. Street after street; and all the folks asleep—street after street, all lighted up as if for a procession and all as empty as a church—till at last I got into that state of mind when a man listens and listens and begins to long for the sight of a policeman. All at once, I saw two figures: one a little man who was stumping along eastward at a good walk, and the other a girl of maybe eight or ten who was running as hard as she was able down a cross street. Well, sir, the two ran into one another naturally enough at the corner; and then came the horrible part of the thing; for the man trampled calmly over the child's body and left her screaming on the ground. It sounds nothing to hear, but it was hellish to see. It wasn't like a man; it was like some damned Juggernaut. I gave a view-halloa, took to my heels, collared my gentleman, and brought him back to where there was already quite a group about the screaming...

Chapter 9: Reading with the Brain

We now know a little about the physical processes the brain uses to accomplish the task of reading, but how can we make the most of this ability? What mental processes should we be using to best convert text into knowledge? Where's the "User's Guide" for this reading machine?

As you have probably noticed, there is already plenty of advice available on reading techniques.

In fact, having so much advice can make it difficult to decide which advice is excellent and which is nonsense. Our previous discussion of how we process text, however, may help you determine which methods make more sense.

The last chapter primarily dealt with how the brain converts printed text into words, but this chapter will concentrate on how these words are turned into meaning. We will cover how words are turned into the thoughts they came from, and how language becomes ideas. We will also look closer at how the right brain can enhance this ability.

Perceptual and Conceptual Processing

Once text enters your brain, it is processed in two stages: perceptual and conceptual.

The first processing stage is perceptual; this is when you see text and recognize the characters and words. As amazing as this ability is, it is actually the simpler and faster of the two stages.

Of course, the whole reading process seems incredibly fast when you consider the complexity involved, but the second stage, the conceptual stage, is by far the slower of the two. A whole phrase of text can be perceived in about 1/25th of a second. That's very fast—around seven times faster than you can blink!

That means a group of words can be flashed on a screen so fast as to be almost invisible, but you can still perceive the whole phrase. However, conceptualizing the meaning of that phrase takes considerably longer.

To understand how much longer it takes to actually read and understand text, consider that even reading at a rapid six hundred words per minute is equivalent to spending an entire half a second on each phrase. In other words, the *thinking* part of reading takes over ten times longer than the *seeing* part.

This huge difference between the time it takes to perceive text and the time it takes to conceptually process it should make it abundantly clear why speed reading has nothing to do with *seeing* text faster, but everything to do with *thinking* faster. Speed reading is really speed thinking.

That's why it is pointless to push the speed of seeing text, regardless if it's with eye exercises or by following a pacer. Eyes are not cameras. The "camera" is the whole brain, and the eyes are only the lens of this camera.

The eyes are an important component, but useless without the complex mechanisms required for processing and saving information.

Reading is a complex process involving various operations. The whole process takes visual input, converts it to lines and shapes, then to letters and words, to language, and then to data. It next filters and sorts this data into information, and then finally saves it as useful knowledge. The entire process involves several simultaneous and integrated tasks, working together to generate new thoughts and memories.

These thoughts and memories are the final result and sole purpose of all this work; a process which allows you to categorize, organize, store, and recall what you have read. As you can see, the end result of a system like this is knowledge, not memorization. This means the purpose of reading is *not* to remember words, but to assimilate *ideas*.

The purpose of conceptually understanding information is to make the information *useful*. The brain is a predicting and planning machine, and it uses categorizations and connections of stored information to accomplish those tasks.

Episodic and Semantic Information

There are two types of information: episodic and semantic.

Episodic information is located in time and space. These are concrete things—things that are in the real world and can be observed.

Semantic information is outside of time and space. These are abstract things—things you can only understand as conceptual ideas and things that can only be represented as categories and connections.

Consider the sentence, "He was running faster than ever." "He was running" is episodic information, and "faster than ever" is semantic. The first phrase is a concrete image. The second phrase is an abstract idea.

When conceptualizing what you read, episodic information is somewhat faster and easier to imagine than semantic information, as it is easier to think of real world things than abstract ideas. Without any visual image, semantic information requires more imagination and mental effort to process.

But although the processing of semantic information takes more effort, it is one of the abilities which make us uniquely human—and it beats the opposable thumbs, hands down! Chimps, for example, cannot effectively process semantic information, meaning they have very little ability to reason about unobservable things. But semantically thinking humans can understand how the past affects the present and then how to use this understanding to plan for the future.

Consciousness

Once data is processed into conceptual ideas, it is presented to the conscious mind. Here the data is quickly filtered by tuning out what is not important, and amplifying what is. This is also where you become aware of the data as information.

Although the conscious portion of the brain is small, it acts as the boss, delegating tasks and receiving reports from all the subconscious areas. As information streams through the conscious mind, it is temporarily placed in the short-term working memory, where it is analyzed, combined, compared, and evaluated. Although the short- term memory can't hold many items or hold them for long—since each conscious item can be immensely complex—it can still handle a large amount of information. Because it takes about the same amount of effort to process a large concept as it does an individual word, concentrating on reading for ideas can maximize the processing speed.

Another way consciousness maximizes its efficiency is by filtering out anything it thinks is irrelevant, enabling it to concentrate more time and energy on what matters most. You could think of this as a secretary going through and prioritizing the incoming mail. Not everything that comes in escapes the wastebasket, but the most important items go to the top of the inbox.

The result of this filtering is that you won't remember everything you read—and you wouldn't want to; that's not how the brain is supposed to work. The brain is more like an index than a book. Its job is not to simply record its experiences, but to organize and make sense of them.

Memory

After the data has been filtered and evaluated, the information is stored in the long-term memory. This information is not stored in one place, but distributed throughout a network of associated attributes. Each of these attributes is like a tag associated with the information and represents a quality or characteristic inherent in that information.

Instead of being stored as intact bundles, this information is saved as a set of related attributes. Each piece of information is not stored as a separate block somewhere in the brain, but as a complex web of connections to all associated information. In this way, we store memories of what information actually means to us. The result is that unlike a computer, we don't store "data"—we store knowledge. In other words, we don't store the exact information or experience, but instead store the conceptual *idea* of that information.

This also explains why memories change over time. It is not because we forget them; it's because we never really remembered them in the first place, at least not as exact recordings of facts and events. In fact, the latest studies on memory have found that memories are actually altered every time they are recalled, depending on which attributes are connected and which attributes are more strongly emphasized.

This understanding of memory will increase your reading efficiency by encouraging you to concentrate on the conceptual phrases rather than trying to memorize the words and details. Unless you are trying to memorize something like technical jargon or a poem, you are not remembering the words, but the ideas. Comprehending text means thinking of what it means.

Here's an example of conceptualizing via attributes. The thought of a red rose creates attribute connections for red things, roses, flowers, plants, and any other categories you might associate with a red rose—including any emotional attachment you might associate with roses. Later on when you retrieve this information, you aren't really retrieving the original memory; you are instead reconstructing the memory from a distributed network of attributes, where each attribute contributes to the larger meaning of the idea. When you remember this information, you will recreate this memory as red + rose + flower + plant, including, excluding, and even replacing many of these puzzle pieces from all the connections that were originally made.

The point is, each memory is actually distributed throughout a network of connections to many other memories; these memories will be stronger or weaker based on the number and strength of these connections, and then will be further affected by the number of times they are accessed.

Over time, the more you know about red roses, the more connection points you will have established and will be available for similar information to be attached to. Every additional piece of information you store will make it faster and easier to store new pieces. This will also make information faster and easier to retrieve since there will be more connection points to access it from. For example, just thinking of "red" might remind you of that particular rose and the occasion of that memory.

Another variable that affects the memory process is age. For instance, the reason we don't form long-term memories before the age of three is probably because we don't yet have enough memories to firmly attach new information to. If an infant sees a table for the first time and then later sees a chair, the chair will not remind him of the previous table because no conceptual connections have been made between these two items yet. The table will be easily forgotten, as well as the chair and any other memories associated with either of these items.

But by the time we have accumulated about three years of experiences, we will have created enough associations to begin to make connections strong enough to possibly last for years.

Then later, after a certain age, the brain begins to suffer a slowdown in processing speed. But due to neuroplasticity, the brain can compensate for some of this slowdown by making use of the many more connection points available, the larger vocabulary, and the sharper language skills developed by that time.

Regardless of age, though, the more you read, the more you exercise your brain. Furthermore, the more you put into your brain, the richer life becomes.

Concentration and Focus

Knowing how the brain reads and how to improve its functioning is important, but this knowledge is useless until put into practice. Knowledge is not power—it is only *potential* power. Power requires effort. All reading and comprehension takes mental effort, and trying to read and comprehend faster will obviously require an increased effort. Most of this additional effort will be directed to paying more *attention*; which involves an increase in *concentration* and *focus*.

"Concentration" is applying more mental resources to your reading, it's thinking more about what the information means. Increased concentration is like shining a brighter light on a subject. In this way, concentrating on your reading makes the information clearer and easier to see.

"Focus" is tuning out internal or external distractions in order to narrow your attention to the material at hand. Focus increases your mental efficiency by minimizing the waste of resources. Increased focus is like looking at the subject through a magnifying glass, as it strengthens attention on the information being read and reduces attention to distractions.

One way to maximize the overall mental energy you have available for these tasks, is to be sure your brain is operating in top condition. A good way to do this is by providing your brain with adequate fuel— and it uses *lots* of fuel. Amazingly, although the brain only makes up two percent of the body's total weight, it uses twenty-five percent of the body's oxygen and seventy percent of its glucose. The best way to ensure a good fuel supply is through good health; so for maximum efficiency, it's very helpful if you get proper physical exercise, nutrition, and rest.

Even though there are limits to the improvements that can be made to your brain, you can still strengthen it with mental exercise. In fact, practicing to enhance your reading abilities has a powerful impact, not only on your reading skills, but on your physical brain itself.

Besides increased effort, it also takes *time* to develop better reading skills. You should also be aware that reading whole phrases and concentrating on conceptual ideas as you read is going to feel strange at first; changing old habits usually feels a bit uncomfortable. But if it doesn't feel strange, then you probably aren't doing anything different. So accept that it will take time for your mind to adjust to conceptual reading.

Concentrating on whole thoughts and visualizing and conceptualizing whole ideas uses more of your brain. It spreads these communication tasks over a broader portion of the brain than simply decoding text into words would do. The visual, big-picture area of the right brain specializes in this complex, conceptual type of thinking.

Reading with the Right Brain

Most of the areas of the brain typically associated with reading are on the left side, and this is actually the area we are most familiar with. But the area this book is primarily concerned with is way over on the right. Textual information arrives on the right side via the corpus callosum—a wide, flat bundle of neural fibers connecting the two brain halves.

When you study how the brain reads, you will see a lot of information about processes and areas of the left brain. Over on the right side, it's much more of an unexplored frontier. In fact, this side seems to get a lot less attention overall. For example, if you do a Google search for pictures of the brain, you'll see that almost all the images are of the left side.

The left hemisphere is where our language center is located—this is the side that talks to us. Maybe that's the reason it's so much easier to get to know than the silent right side.

But the right side actually has a major role in effective comprehension. The right side is where concepts and visual images are formed.

The difference between the two hemispheres was first discovered when patients had their corpora callosa severed in attempts to eliminate severe epileptic seizures. Doctors found that when these people were shown words to the left sides of their brains (paradoxically, through their right eyes), the signals were unable to cross to the right sides, and these patients were unable to identify pictures that matched the words. Likewise, if a picture was presented to the right sides of their brains, they were unable to produce the matching words. This lack of communication is what proved to neurologists that the separate hemispheres actually had very different functions.

The right side of the brain thinks by looking at information as complete patterns. Unlike the left side, which processes information in a step-by-step fashion, the right side looks at whole images or whole ideas together and sees the overall patterns and connections of the information.

This unique talent allows the right side to handle the higher order cognitive processing, which means it can interpret information faster, more holistically, and recognize the big picture. This holistic ability is why the right side excels at things like imagination, intuition, facial recognition, and artistry, while the left side can balance a checkbook.

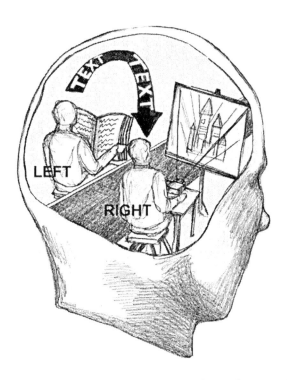

Both sides have their own important specialties, but reading only with the left brain is like squeezing information through a straw, compared to the wide river of information that the right brain can process simultaneously.

After the left and right side process data, it is sent to the prefrontal cortex. This is the seat of consciousness, an area which regulates information, modulates impulses, and coordinates data coming from other brain centers. This area enables you to form plans, make decisions, spot errors, and break habits. It is also where working memory—the mental desktop—resides.

While the prefrontal cortex's job is to process data into meaningful information, there are aspects of information which could affect processing capabilities—emotion, for one thing. Dopamine, the neurotransmitter associated with joy and pleasure, primes the prefrontal cortex for action and strengthens its informational signals. Also assisting the prefrontal cortex in its processing are repeated, rhythmic, structured, and easily visualized information—all of which make information easier to remember.

Practice Exercise #9

As you read this exercise, be aware of what your mind is doing. Reading words may be automatic for you, but this doesn't mean the rest of your brain and consciousness will automatically be involved.

In order for you to get anything lasting out of your reading, it helps to understand how your brain works and which form of information it works with best. This means paying attention to the real conceptual meaning of information, whether it is concrete or abstract. If you want your consciousness to stay involved and store this information into your long-term memory, you must concentrate, focus, and conceptualize.

When you're ready, begin reading the first thousand words of

White Fang by Jack London

White Fang

Dark spruce forest frowned on either side of the frozen waterway. The trees had been stripped by a recent wind of their white covering of frost, and they seemed to lean towards each other, black and ominous, in the fading light. A vast silence reigned over the land. The land itself was a desolation; lifeless, without movement, so lone and cold that the spirit of it was not even that of sadness. There was a hint in it of laughter, but of a laughter more terrible than any sadness—a laughter that was mirthless as the smile of the sphinx, a laughter cold as the frost and partaking of the grimness of infallibility. It was the masterful and incommunicable wisdom of eternity laughing at the futility of life and the effort of life. It was the Wild, the savage, frozen-hearted Northland Wild.

But there was life, abroad in the land and defiant. Down the frozen waterway toiled a string of wolfish dogs. Their bristly fur was rimed with frost. Their breath froze in the air as it left their mouths, spouting forth in spumes of vapor that settled upon the hair of their bodies and formed into crystals of frost. Leather harness was on the dogs, and leather traces attached them to a sled which dragged along behind. The sled was without runners. It was made of stout birch-bark, and its full surface rested on the snow. The front end of the sled was turned up, like a scroll, in order to force down and under the bore of soft snow that surged like a wave before it. On the sled, securely lashed, was a long and narrow oblong box. There were other things on the sled— blankets, an axe, and a coffee-pot and frying-pan; but prominent, occupying most of the space, was the long and narrow oblong box.

In advance of the dogs, on wide snowshoes, toiled a man. At the rear of the sled toiled a second man. On the sled, in the box, lay a third man whose toil was over—a man whom the Wild had conquered and beaten down until he would never move nor struggle again. It is not the way of the Wild to like movement. Life is an offence to it, for life is movement; and the Wild aims always to destroy movement. It freezes the water to prevent it running to the sea; it drives the sap out of the trees till they are frozen to their mighty hearts; and most ferociously and terribly of all does the Wild harry and crush into submission man—man who is the most restless of life, ever in revolt against the dictum that all movement must in the end come to the cessation of movement.

But at front and rear, unawed and indomitable, toiled the two men who were not yet dead. Their bodies were covered with fur and soft-tanned leather. Eyelashes and cheeks and lips were so coated with the crystals from their frozen breath that their faces were not discernible. This gave them the seeming of ghostly masques, undertakers in a spectral world at the funeral of some ghost. But under it all they were men, penetrating the land of desolation and mockery and silence, puny adventurers bent on colossal adventure, pitting themselves against the might of a world as remote and alien and pulseless as the abysses of space.

They traveled on without speech, saving their breath for the work of their bodies. On every side was the silence, pressing upon them with a tangible presence. It affected their minds as the many atmospheres of deep water affect the body of the diver. It crushed them with the weight of unending vastness and unalterable decree. It crushed them into the remotest recesses of their own minds, pressing out of them, like juices from the grape, all the false ardors and exaltations and undue self-values of the human soul, until they perceived themselves finite and small, specks and motes, moving with weak cunning and little wisdom amidst the play and inter-play of the great blind elements and forces.

An hour went by, and a second hour. The pale light of the short sunless day was beginning to fade, when a faint far cry arose on the still air. It soared upward with a swift rush, till it reached its topmost note, where it persisted, palpitant and tense, and then slowly died away. It might have been a lost soul wailing, had it not been invested with a certain sad fierceness and hungry eagerness. The front man turned his head until his eyes met the eyes of the man behind. And then, across the narrow oblong box, each nodded to the other.

A second cry arose, piercing the silence with needle-like shrillness. Both men located the sound. It was to the rear, somewhere in the snow expanse they had just traversed. A third and answering cry arose, also to the rear and to the left of the second cry.

"They're after us, Bill," said the man at the front.

His voice sounded hoarse and unreal, and he had spoken with apparent effort.

"Meat is scarce," answered his comrade. "I ain't seen a rabbit sign for days."

Thereafter they spoke no more, though their ears were keen for the hunting-cries that continued to rise behind them.

At the fall of darkness they swung the dogs into a cluster of spruce trees on the edge of the waterway and made a camp. The coffin, at the side of the fire, served for seat and table. The wolf-dogs, clustered on the far side of the fire, snarled and bickered among themselves, but evinced no inclination to stray off into the darkness.

"Seems to me, Henry, they're stayin' remarkable close to camp," Bill commented.

Henry, squatting over the fire and settling the pot of coffee with a piece of ice, nodded. Nor did he speak till he had taken his seat on the coffin and begun to eat. "They know...

Chapter 10: Mindset

The proper mindset for effective reading requires both, paying more attention, and knowing what to pay attention to. You must also treat your attention like the precious and finite resource it is, and direct it at the real purpose of reading—*comprehension*.

Attention

It might seem that there is something mystical or magical about speed reading, or that it's some awesome ability only a few lucky geniuses have. If this is what you think, then be prepared to go from being amazed to thinking, "What's the big deal? It's only about paying more attention."

And that's the truth; it is only about paying attention. But paying attention is really huge. "Attention" is your conscious mind. If you had zero attention, you would be comatose—barely alive. Having more attention is being more alive. Attention is the "you" in your brain. More attention means more you.

You might think that naturally you are paying attention, but attention is variable. Attention is not stuck at one level, and it's not simply an on and off switch; it's more like a dimmer switch that can be adjusted anywhere between very bright and very dim, and this adjustment varies throughout each day.

The power of attention also varies among different people. Just like any part of the physical body, each person's mental processes can also be stronger or weaker than those of others. You could even conclude that some people are more conscious than others.

But believe it or not, the conscious mind can be strengthened with exercise. With regular reading exercise and good technique, you can stretch your memory, tighten your attention, and strengthen your intelligence. You can also learn to make more efficient use of the working memory of your conscious mind, maintain better concentration and focus, and suppress external and internal distractions.

Here's a simple trick that will increase attention: pretend the reason you are reading something, is to explain it to someone else. Think, "How can I make this information clear? What is the gist of this material? How do the different parts fit together? How could I defend this idea if someone were to disagree with it?" But this really isn't just a trick, because you *are* going to explain it to someone else—your future self.

Improving attention depends a lot on your mindset. In order to make good progress, your mind must be rested, fit, and positive. Imagine if you were at the gym. The first thing you would do is stretch to prepare your muscles and get them warmed up. Likewise, your brain should also be prepared before exercise so it can be in the right frame of mind, ready to concentrate and focus on the job at hand.

Relaxation

Prepare your brain for reading and learning by relaxing your mind and body. Relaxation clears your working memory, erasing that mental white board. Relaxation also calms the amygdala and prefrontal cortex, your emotional and conscious areas. These two areas work closely together and will communicate better when they are undistracted and uncluttered.

The amygdala is the hub of emotional responses and can produce a stimulating effect on the prefrontal cortex. The prefrontal cortex is the seat of executive function; it regulates your thoughts, actions, and emotions. There is a strong connection between these two regions and distractions in one will affect the other. Relaxing your mind clears the communication channel between them.

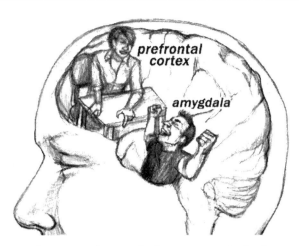

If you're not sure how to relax and clear your mind, then try this. Close your eyes, and think of nothing but your breathing. Then, picture in your mind each letter of the words READ FASTER. Picture them one at a time, and imagine each one inflating and then deflating as you breathe in and then out. This exercise will accomplish two things: it will clear your mind of extraneous distractions, and it will also warm up the visualizing areas of your brain.

Another very easy trick is smiling! Strangely enough, the physical act of putting a smile on your face actually *creates* a positive mood, and a positive mood produces a relaxed and receptive mind. A positive mood even improves your vision, because happy and positive thoughts cause your pupils to dilate, letting in more light.

Purpose

It is also helpful to keep your goals in mind when deciding to read something. Any journey comes with some measure of apprehension. You may wonder: "How long will it take me? Will it be worth it? How will I feel if I fail to achieve this goal?"

Before investing in any goal, we want to know if it's worth the effort by deciding how much effort it will take, what will be gained if we succeed, and what will be lost if we fail. But before we can know how much effort a reading task is worth, we need to be clear about the reading goals.

Having a clear goal will help any reading, regardless whether the goal is to hunt down specific knowledge or just indulge in recreation. Realize what you want, what it is worth, what it will cost you, and what you would be giving up if you forfeited it. Being clear about your goal will clear the road ahead, enabling you to focus undistracted attention on your reading, regardless of whether you're reading a difficult textbook or a trashy novel.

All reading has a purpose because it all adds knowledge—either knowledge of the world as it exists, or of its possibilities—either increasing your intelligence, or your empathy. And all knowledge changes you, because you literally become more of what you read. So decide on your reason for reading and read with motivation. Then read aggressively by actively seeking the information, not just waiting for it to occur to you.

Patience

It's also important to be patient with yourself. Don't be overly concerned about how long it's taking you to finish reading something. Your attention is limited, so pay attention to what you are doing right now rather than how far you are from the end. You've set your course, now keep your eyes on the road directly in front of you. Ignore the little voice in the back of your mind asking, "Are we there yet? Are we there yet?" Worrying about your progress only leads to performance anxiety. You know where you're going; you know how to get there. Now, relax and enjoy the scenery. Be patient. Your goal is to read and understand the material, so concentrate on visualizing the information, and you will get there faster.

You should also accept that you still may not always understand everything you read. But when you come across something that is troublesome, stop and see if you can figure out why it is giving you a problem. If it is still not clear, then make note of it, continue reading, and see if it becomes clear later.

Practice Exercise #10

As you read this next practice exercise, relax, be patient, and concentrate on imagining what you are reading. Attention, relaxation, purpose, and patience are important ingredients, although these should not require your conscious effort. By concentrating on the conceptual nature of what you read, you will automatically be paying more attention, be more relaxed and read with purpose and patience. You will be filling your mind with conceptual ideas, and therefore will just naturally avoid distractions, tension, confusion, and impatience.

Once again, remember to time your reading and record your words per minute on your progress form. Even though you are concentrating more on comprehension than speed, your speed is still a helpful indirect indication of your progress.

When you're ready, begin reading the first thousand words of

***Memoirs of Sherlock Holmes* by Sir Arthur Conan Doyle**

Memoirs of Sherlock Holmes

"I am afraid, Watson, that I shall have to go," said Holmes, as we sat down together to our breakfast one morning.

"Go! Where to?"

"To Dartmoor; to King's Pyland."

I was not surprised. Indeed, my only wonder was that he had not already been mixed up in this extraordinary case, which was the one topic of conversation through the length and breadth of England. For a whole day my companion had rambled about the room with his chin upon his chest and his brows knitted, charging and recharging his pipe with the strongest black tobacco, and absolutely deaf to any of my questions or remarks. Fresh editions of every paper had been sent up by our news agent, only to be glanced over and tossed down into a corner. Yet, silent as he was, I knew perfectly well what it was over which he was brooding. There was but one problem before the public which could challenge his powers of analysis, and that was the singular disappearance of the favorite for the Wessex Cup, and the tragic murder of its trainer. When, therefore, he suddenly announced his intention of setting out for the scene of the drama it was only what I had both expected and hoped for.

"I should be most happy to go down with you if I should not be in the way," said I.

"My dear Watson, you would confer a great favor upon me by coming. And I think that your time will not be misspent, for there are points about the case which promise to make it an absolutely unique one. We have, I think, just time to catch our train at Paddington, and I will go further into the matter upon our journey. You would oblige me by bringing with you your very excellent field-glass."

And so it happened that an hour or so later I found myself in the corner of a first-class carriage flying along en route for Exeter, while Sherlock Holmes, with his sharp, eager face framed in his ear-flapped travelling-cap, dipped rapidly into the bundle of fresh papers which he had procured at Paddington. We had left Reading far behind us before he thrust the last one of them under the seat, and offered me his cigar-case.

"We are going well," said he, looking out the window and glancing at his watch. "Our rate at present is fifty-three and a half miles an hour."

"I have not observed the quarter-mile posts," said I.

"Nor have I. But the telegraph posts upon this line are sixty yards apart, and the calculation is a simple one. I presume that you have looked into this matter of the murder of John Straker and the disappearance of Silver Blaze?"

"I have seen what the Telegraph and the Chronicle have to say."

"It is one of those cases where the art of the reasoner should be used rather for the sifting of details than for the acquiring of fresh evidence. The tragedy has been so uncommon, so complete and of such personal importance to so many people, that we are suffering from a plethora of surmise, conjecture, and hypothesis. The difficulty is to detach the framework of fact—of absolute undeniable fact—from the embellishments of theorists and reporters. Then, having established ourselves upon this sound basis, it is our duty to see what inferences may be drawn and what are the special points upon which the whole mystery turns. On Tuesday evening I received telegrams from both Colonel Ross, the owner of the horse, and from Inspector Gregory, who is looking after the case, inviting my cooperation."

"Tuesday evening!" I exclaimed. "And this is Thursday morning. Why didn't you go down yesterday?"

"Because I made a blunder, my dear Watson—which is, I am afraid, a more common occurrence than any one would think who only knew me through your memoirs. The fact is that I could not believe it possible that the most remarkable horse in England could long remain concealed, especially in so sparsely inhabited a place as the north of Dartmoor. From hour to hour yesterday I expected to hear that he had been found, and that his abductor was the murderer of John Straker. When, however, another morning had come, and I found that beyond the arrest of young Fitzroy Simpson nothing had been done, I felt that it was time for me to take action. Yet in some ways I feel that yesterday has not been wasted."

"You have formed a theory, then?"

"At least I have got a grip of the essential facts of the case. I shall enumerate them to you, for nothing clears up a case so much as stating it to another person, and I can hardly expect your co-operation if I do not show you the position from which we start."

I lay back against the cushions, puffing at my cigar, while Holmes, leaning forward, with his long, thin forefinger checking off the points upon the palm of his left hand, gave me a sketch of the events which had led to our journey.

"Silver Blaze," said he, "is from the Somomy stock, and holds as brilliant a record as his famous ancestor. He is now in his fifth year, and has brought in turn each of the prizes of the turf to Colonel Ross, his fortunate owner. Up to the time of the catastrophe he was the first favorite for the Wessex Cup, the betting being three to one on him. He has always, however, been a prime favorite with the racing public, and has never yet disappointed them, so that even at those odds enormous sums of money have been laid upon him. It is obvious, therefore, that there were many people who had the strongest interest in preventing Silver Blaze from being there at the fall of the flag next Tuesday.

"The fact was, of course, appreciated at King's Pyland, where the Colonel's training-stable is situated. Every precaution was taken to guard...

Chapter 11: Comprehension

I don't know why, but few people seem to recognize that we are not trying to read WORDS—we are trying to read IDEAS.

Reading is all about comprehension. Reading without comprehension is like reading with your eyes closed. Comprehension means more than just understanding words and definitions; it means understanding the ideas being communicated.

Comprehension depends on the writer and the reader; it is a connection between two minds, and good comprehension depends on both ends of this connection.

Since comprehension is the purpose of text, it would be helpful to consider what comprehension is, what affects it, and how to maximize it.

Reading IS Comprehension

Sure, we all know comprehension is important. We want to read faster while maintaining good comprehension. But this is looking at the process completely backwards. Comprehension is the goal of reading and the only reason for reading. It is not a part of reading to be simply *maintained*. What you really want to have is good comprehension... and then also have fast reading.

Even though it seems obvious to everyone that comprehension is important, most reading improvement courses not only ignore comprehension, but even actively discourage it. We are told we can ignore comprehension while pressing ahead with our "reading" speed. We are told that *after* we develop the habit of seeing words faster, our comprehension will somehow catch up. I'm afraid it just doesn't work like that, as you have probably discovered for yourself.

Pushing your speed and expecting your comprehension to catch up is like flooring the accelerator on your car and expecting your driving skills to catch up. Your car would soon crash as certainly as your comprehension would.

Comprehension is a skill, a complex mental skill that doesn't improve on its own. Like most skills, you have to master proper technique before you can perform the skill faster. Improved comprehension is what leads to speed, not vice versa.

Not only does comprehension fail to automatically improve with faster reading, it is also possible to read words and have absolutely no comprehension at all. How often have you read an entire page with your mind on autopilot, only to discover that you didn't remember a thing?

Here's another example of "reading" without understanding. Even though I do not *understand* Spanish, the phonetic rules of the language are logical enough that I could probably *say* all the words. This means I could read a Spanish book aloud and most Spanish speaking people would understand what I was saying. But just because I could say the words wouldn't mean I was actually reading them. I would only be decoding written symbols into their associated sounds. In the end, I am not taking away any information, just sounds. This is the same if I were to read English while ignoring comprehension. Comprehension must come first—without it, you aren't really *reading* at all.

The path to faster reading is *improving comprehension by conceptualizing meaning*. By following this path, your reading speed will increase automatically—a natural result of faster understanding. With more effective comprehension, you'll not only read faster, but you'll have more to show for it.

Information Density

The information density of a piece of text depends on how much new information is contained within that text, and this can have a huge effect on comprehension. Data that contains no new information is the easiest to read because most of this empty data will be simply discarded by the prefrontal cortex.

But after this filtering, data that includes new information is going to go through additional processing to be sorted, prioritized, and finally connected to previous knowledge through shared attributes.

During this process, some of the knowledge may be deemed interesting enough to require further contemplation, in which case you may even halt your reading momentarily to ponder and examine this important discovery and make further mental attachments.

Imagine your reading to be like walking through a museum. You move quickly past displays you've seen before, slow down to consider those new and interesting items, and then sometimes stop and stare at the most surprising finds.

Information density also affects your ability to stay connected with the material and to prevent your mind from wandering. Since the prefrontal cortex tries to be energy efficient, it attempts to ignore low density information.

When information density is too low, you will have a tendency to begin skimming the text, which will make it harder to keep your mind firmly connected with it. However, when information density is too high, you may be forced to slow down so much that it can become difficult to keep the larger picture of the information in your mind.

Being aware of how information density changes and affects your comprehension will help you accommodate these changes by accepting a constantly changing reading speed.

Information Attachment

Conceptualizing information is still not the very end of the reading process. Information that is not attached to previous knowledge will quickly evaporate and disappear. Information attachment takes place via attributes the new information shares with existing information. Do you enjoy a sport or a hobby? If you do, you will easily remember a new record or achievement in that field.

Your current personal knowledge base was built out of those things you found interesting in the past. This existing knowledge is what supplies attachment points for new related information. Your interest in a subject will improve your comprehension because you will have many other pieces of related information with which to quickly associate and attach new information. It is literally true to describe an interest as an "attachment" to the subject, because new information about the subject will easily find more attachments to your existing knowledge.

Furthermore, if you have a larger number of interests, there will be more subjects that will be easier and more interesting to read about. This actually creates a virtuous circle: the more you know about each subject, the more interesting it becomes; and then the more interesting it becomes, the more you'll want to know about it. This is a terrific cure for boredom. In fact, when something seems boring, it's often not the material that's boring—it's us.

Developing more interest in a subject will also change your reading from passive to aggressive. You will find that you will tend to aggressively seek information as you read about these subjects, rather than passively wait for ideas to occur to you.

Phrase Attachment

Another form of information attachment is the attachment between the phrases in each sentence. Each of these meaningful phrases will attach to the prior and next phrases, and your comprehension will depend on these bonds. Although it's easier and faster to comprehend words in meaningful groups than one at a time, these groups also become more meaningful in the context of their neighboring groups.

For example, you will notice that when you first start reading something, your comprehension may start off feeling weak and tenuous, but then it begins to strengthen as you continue reading. This is because each phrase you encounter is assisting those around it by supplying additional supporting context. Each new piece of information elaborates on the preceding piece and then narrows the possibilities of what's coming next.

This takes effect, whether you are starting a book, a chapter, a page, a paragraph, or even a sentence. It takes a bit of effort to get traction as you encounter each new idea. Let's walk part way through a sentence to demonstrate this. Consider this sentence:

"Now, as it turned out, the Rebellion was achieved much earlier and more easily than anyone had expected."

Dividing this into phrases could look like this:

Now, as it turned out, the Rebellion was achieved much earlier and more easily than anyone had expected.

When you come across the first phrase, *"Now,"* it would appear that this is likely some kind of exclamatory statement, but otherwise the meaning would still be pretty vague.

But the next phrase, *"as it turned out,"* adds to the meaning of *"Now,"* which now appears to indicate *when* something *turned out*. And not only does the second phrase add to the meaning of the first, it also gives a clue as to what the next phrase might be about. It doesn't tell you *what* the next phrase is going to be, but it narrows the list of likely possibilities. This makes the third phrase easier to understand because you know it will be limited to something that will make sense in the context of the previous phrase.

Next, when you come to *"the Rebellion,"* the same principle applies. This phrase clarifies the information of the preceding phrase and again narrows the possibilities of the following phrase. We now know, *"as it turned out,"* refers to some rebellion; additionally, we know that the upcoming phrase will probably describe something about the rebellion.

While this has been a rather long-winded description, the whole process occurs in microseconds. The mental process of attaching phrases to one another is so fast as to be almost unconscious, but it's important to understand that the phrases and ideas are parts of a chain. Reading should be a smooth stream of comprehension, with each piece fitting into its neighbors in a continuous flow of information in context. Therefore, your comprehension will usually start out slower as you collect this context and then accelerate as the information becomes more meaningful and the larger ideas emerge.

A good metaphor for this process is thoughts connected by a string. First, you have to be sure you have a firm grip on the string; then, you can gradually start to pull, and the rest of the string will come along. But if you yank too hard or too quickly, your mental string will break and your comprehension will slip away. Also, some sections of a string may be more fragile than others, which means you will have to pull more slowly and carefully to maintain comprehension.

Since it takes a bit of reading to first develop a context for the material and to understand what it is about, it's important that you are willing to let your reading be slower at first and then speed up on its own as the larger ideas materialize around this context.

Flow

Another thing that affects reading comprehension is writing style. Writing that flows well, that just seems more natural, is always a lot easier to understand. If the author's words have a natural rhythm and they flow well, it will take less mental energy for you to translate the writing back into ideas, leaving you more energy left for processing those ideas.

Good writing flow is an important factor in reading comprehension. Good flow probably has more impact on comprehension than sentence length or vocabulary. Unfortunately, good flow is not easily achievable for writers; few excel at creating it. Below are two sentences to compare. Both are examples of good writing, taken from famous novels; but one flows better than the other.

From *The Velveteen Rabbit:*

For at least two hours the Boy loved him, and then Aunts and Uncles came to dinner, and there was a great rustling of tissue paper and unwrapping of parcels, and in the excitement of looking at all the new presents the Velveteen Rabbit was forgotten.

From *The Jungle Book:*

Mother Wolf lay with her big gray nose dropped across her four tumbling, squealing cubs, and the moon shone into the mouth of the cave where they all lived.

Although both examples contain good writing, you will probably notice that the first one seems to *flow* better—it's somehow just a little easier to understand. This is true even though the first sentence is longer, and its words are no shorter or easier than the second sentence.

The difference here is flow. Flow has to do with the flow of ideas—either through time or from big picture to detail. Good writing flow progresses logically, the way we think. It is easier to understand a sentence that describes a period of time if it moves from past to future, rather than backwards as a series of flashbacks. It is also easier to understand a sentence that describes a scene if it starts with the overall image and then zooms in on the details, rather than focusing on multiple minutiae and making us wait to see what they add up to.

The first example above flows from one moment in time to the next in a logical fashion, making it easy for us to understand where the ideas are going.

The second example moves through space—instead of time—but from detail to big picture, rather than vice versa; so that we need to hold the details in mind until the whole picture emerges.

The result of good flow is that it takes the reader carefully through the information, ensuring the short-term memory is never overburdened with unsupported moments in time or unattached fragments of a scene. With good flow, each new piece of information is easily and logically associated with the prior piece, and the reader is not required to wait to assemble the pieces like a jigsaw puzzle at the conclusion of the sentence.

Being aware of density, attachment, and flow means actively maintaining a balance between speed and comprehension. A lot of things can affect your comprehension. Allowing your speed to fluctuate not only allows for better comprehension, but it even helps maintain your attention. If you read at a constant, mechanical, unchanging speed, it can be like listening to a boring, monotone speaker. So mix it up. Slow your pace when necessary, and be ready to sprint when you can.

Practice Exercise #11

Read this next exercise, making sure that you are concentrating on comprehension. See each idea because this is key to getting the right brain involved. The right brain doesn't understand words, it understands ideas. But feed it ideas only as fast as it can handle them—no faster, but no slower. Remember, it's your comprehension speed that you want to maximize, not just words per minute.

When you're ready, begin reading the first thousand words of

The Voyages of Dr. Dolittle by Hugh Lofting

The Voyages of Dr. Dolittle

My name was Tommy Stubbins, son of Jacob Stubbins, the cobbler of Puddleby-on-the-Marsh; and I was nine and a half years old. At that time Puddleby was only quite a small town. A river ran through the middle of it; and over this river there was a very old stone bridge, called Kingsbridge, which led you from the market-place on one side to the churchyard on the other.

Sailing-ships came up this river from the sea and anchored near the bridge. I used to go down and watch the sailors unloading the ships upon the river-wall. The sailors sang strange songs as they pulled upon the ropes; and I learned these songs by heart. And I would sit on the river-wall with my feet dangling over the water and sing with the men, pretending to myself that I too was a sailor.

For I longed always to sail away with those brave ships when they turned their backs on Puddleby Church and went creeping down the river again, across the wide lonely marshes to the sea. I longed to go with them out into the world to seek my fortune in foreign lands— Africa, India, China and Peru! When they got round the bend in the river and the water was hidden from view, you could still see their huge brown sails towering over the roofs of the town, moving onward slowly—like some gentle giants that walked among the houses without noise. What strange things would they have seen, I wondered, when next they came back to anchor at Kingsbridge! And, dreaming of the lands I had never seen, I'd sit on there, watching till they were out of sight.

Three great friends I had in Puddleby in those days. One was Joe, the mussel-man, who lived in a tiny hut by the edge of the water under the bridge. This old man was simply marvelous at making things. I never saw a man so clever with his hands. He used to mend my toy ships for me, which I sailed upon the river; he built windmills out of packing-cases and barrel-staves; and he could make the most wonderful kites from old umbrellas.

Joe would sometimes take me in his mussel-boat, and when the tide was running out we would paddle down the river as far as the edge of the sea to get mussels and lobsters to sell. And out there on the cold lonely marshes we would see wild geese flying, and curlews and redshanks and many other kinds of seabirds that live among the samphire and the long grass of the great salt fen. And as we crept up the river in the evening, when the tide had turned, we would see the lights on Kingsbridge twinkle in the dusk, reminding us of tea-time and warm fires.

Another friend I had was Matthew Mugg, the cat's-meat-man. He was a funny old person with a bad squint. He looked rather awful but he was really quite nice to talk to. He knew everybody in Puddleby; and he knew all the dogs and all the cats. In those times being a cat's-meat-man was a regular business. And you could see one nearly any day going through the streets with a wooden tray full of pieces of meat stuck on skewers crying, "Meat! M-E-A-T!" People paid him to give this meat to their cats and dogs instead of feeding them on dog-biscuits or the scraps from the table.

I enjoyed going round with old Matthew and seeing the cats and dogs come running to the garden-gates whenever they heard his call. Sometimes he let me give the meat to the animals myself; and I thought this was great fun. He knew a lot about dogs and he would tell me the names of the different kinds as we went through the town. He had several dogs of his own; one, a whippet, was a very fast runner, and Matthew used to win prizes with her at the Saturday coursing races; another, a terrier, was a fine ratter. The cat's-meat-man used to make a business of rat-catching for the millers and farmers as well as his other trade of selling cat's-meat.

My third great friend was Luke the Hermit. But of him I will tell you more later on.

I did not go to school; because my father was not rich enough to send me. But I was extremely fond of animals. So I used to spend my time collecting birds' eggs and butterflies, fishing in the river, rambling through the countryside after blackberries and mushrooms and helping the mussel-man mend his nets.

Yes, it was a very pleasant life I lived in those days long ago—though of course I did not think so then. I was nine and a half years old; and, like all boys, I wanted to grow up—not knowing how well off I was with no cares and nothing to worry me. Always I longed for the time when I should be allowed to leave my father's house, to take passage in one of those brave ships, to sail down the river through the misty marshes to the sea—out into the world to seek my fortune.

One early morning in the springtime, when I was wandering among the hills at the back of the town, I happened to come upon a hawk with a squirrel in its claws. It was standing on a rock and the squirrel was fighting very hard for its life. The hawk was so frightened when I came upon it suddenly like this, that it dropped the poor creature and flew away. I picked the squirrel up and found that two of its legs were badly hurt. So I carried it in my arms back to the town.

When I came to the bridge I went into the musselman's hut and asked him if he could do anything for it. Joe put on his spectacles and examined it carefully. Then he shook his head.

"Yon crittur's got a broken leg," he said— "and another badly cut an' all. I can mend you your boats, Tom, but I haven't the tools nor the learning to make broken squirrel seaworthy. This is a job for a surgeon—and for a right smart one an' all. There be only...

Chapter 12: Habits

Do you think bad habits are causing you to be a slow reader?

Do you think your reading would improve if you could stop those bad habits?

What are these habits?

- Subvocalizing?
- Regression?
- Mind-wandering?

Of course these things are *associated* with slow reading, but are they the *cause*?

Or are they just *symptoms*?

Subvocalizing

Subvocalizing is the internal speech that we often do when reading. Even when not making a sound, or even moving our lips, there is often a tendency to still at least say the words in our heads.

But why do we subvocalize? Is it really true that it's just a habit we picked up in third grade when our teachers asked us to read aloud? Maybe it started out that way, but I'm sure there are plenty of habits from third grade we, thankfully, no longer have. So why would we still have this one?

First of all, subvocalizing is only a symptom of poor comprehension, but it also develops into a habit. It's more than just a habit though; we hang on to subvocalization because it's a *useful* habit! This is because it's an effective way of *increasing comprehension*. When something is difficult to understand, it can be a big help to verbalize it internally—or even out loud. This verbalizing accomplishes two things:

1. The additional sensation of sound makes information stick in our minds better.

2. Verbalizing automatically adds intonations that divide information into meaningful packets.

Both of these are very helpful for improving comprehension.

The additional sensation of sound (even internally) makes a stronger impression on our conscious mind and short-term memory. Our conscious mind pays more attention when it hears something, and spoken words also seem to stick around longer in our short-term memory.

Sounding out text also helps you listen for subtle changes in pitch that we normally use in speech. When we speak, we involuntarily add vocal inflections to our words. Changes in pitch are automatically used to indicate where each segment of thought begins. These intonations are done so naturally that we are usually unaware of them—they just happen as we speak sentences the way we think they *ought* to sound.

As an example, verbalize the following sentence:

Listen carefully—to the first word—of each phrase.

This is not the only way you could divide this sentence, but however you divide it, you will verbally indicate where you want each phrase to begin, by slightly lowering your pitch on the first word of the phrase. Lowering your pitch does not mean speaking more quietly or with less stress, but simply dropping your pitch to a lower note.

On a musical scale, the intonation would rise and fall something like this:

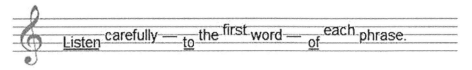

The lower tone of the underlined words indicates to the listener that this is the beginning of a new piece of information, a new phrase. These audio clues are obviously not available in text, so we have a tendency to verbalize to ourselves when we read so that we can then listen for them. This process helps us break sentences into bite-size, meaningful phrases, to make the sentences easier to understand.

So subvocalizing is actually a tool, more than a habit. Or in this case, since it also slows us down, this tool could be considered more of a crutch.

But you'll find the more you visualize and focus on the real meaning of what you read, the less you will want to subvocalize. You won't even have to try not to—you just won't need it. It's hard to know for sure if subvocalizing completely goes away or if you just don't notice it anymore, but you'll begin ignoring sounds and even words. They will be banished as irrelevant thoughts. The sounds will fade away, the words will become invisible, and you will only be aware of ideas and concepts.

Of course, verbalizing will still remain an occasional part of your reading—in some reading more than others. For example, verbalizing is always useful when learning new words. When you first learned to read, all the words were new, but of course you are no longer just recognizing words—you're now recognizing *ideas*.

Regression

Regression is simply going back and rereading. There are two types of regression:

1. Backward saccades
2. Mind-wandering

Saccades are just eye movements. The eyes do not move smoothly over text, but in imperceptibly quick little jerking motions. These are saccades. A backward saccade is when the eyes, which normally move from left to right, jump back to the left again. With an average reader, about one out of four saccades is a jump backward. It's an automatic response to try to make more sense of a current piece of text by jumping back to reconnect it within the context of prior text.

The second type of regression is when you go back even further, several words or sentences. You do this because you either didn't clearly understand something, or your mind temporarily found something more interesting to think about, or you just noticed the text was no longer registering—your mind "blanked out." When this happens, you need to go back far enough to pick up the thread of the topic again.

You can't just blame your disobedient mind for regression. Maybe your mind had nothing to do and simply got bored. Your mind is made for thinking; it's all it does. If you give it nonsense, something it doesn't understand, or something repetitive or boring, it will likely look for something else to think about.

If you are reading with poor comprehension, you simply can't expect your mind to continue paying attention. If your reading is all sound and no content, what can you expect? Who could pay attention to "blah, blah, blah" without falling asleep or wandering off?

Just like verbalizing, both types of regression are also only symptoms. Regression is no more a habit than bending down to pick up a dropped wallet. You bend down and pick up the wallet only because you previously dropped it. Rather than trying to break the "habit" of bending down, you would try to stop dropping the wallet in the first place.

To stop regressing, you must stop your reason for doing it. And what causes regression is reading without comprehension. Regression will stop automatically when you conceptually understand the ideas and make meaningful connections to the information you are reading.

Concentrate on concepts and ideas. Read with purpose and curiosity. It's up to you to make your reading interesting enough for your mind to pay attention to it.

Replace Bad Habits

It's always difficult to concentrate on NOT doing something. Don't yawn. Don't itch. Don't look down. Don't think of a blue elephant. Trying to not do something often has the opposite affect by drawing more attention to the thing you're trying not to do.

When I was learning to ride a motorcycle, I discovered how riders tend to "steer" with their eyes. For example, if you see a road hazard you want to avoid, you have a natural tendency to stare at it. It's obviously dangerous, so you don't want to let it out of your sight. The problem is that staring at it will actually make you steer towards it. I learned to always look where I wanted to go, not where I didn't want to go, and the motorcycle would automatically take me where I was looking. This led to a more effective way to steer on twisting mountain roads. I would keep my eye on a section of road ahead, and that is where the bike would go.

Your mind follows your attention, whether it's positive or negative. Thinking about your bad habits only strengthens them. Instead of thinking about what you *don't* want to do, think about what you *do* want to do.

Concentrating on stopping bad habits is also distracting because it's one more thing to think about. You can't really think of two things at the same time. You are either thinking about what you are reading or thinking about stopping a habit.

Focus on the ideas and that is where your mind will go. Try to visualize and imagine what you read. Picture the ideas and conceptualize what the text is saying. Think about what it means. This will make the ideas behind the text more meaningful and easier and faster to understand. It will make it almost unavoidable to read faster.

So far we've discussed skills, history, and the brain. This big picture, conceptual understanding of how and why reading with the right brain works should give you a meaningful context for the techniques to be discussed in the next two chapters.

But you don't need to really think about all these things while you are reading. That is one of the beauties of reading for meaning. You don't need to concentrate on a lot of rules, tricks, and tips. You only need to concentrate on imagining the ideas you are reading. Concentrate on seeing the meaning, and your mind will do the rest.

Practice Exercise #12

In this next practice exercise, instead of thinking about eliminating *bad* habits, think about creating *new* habits. No concentration should be wasted. Just think about seeing the meaning of what you're reading, and let all the rest naturally take care of itself. Relax, ignore the bad habits, and let them go away on their own.

Imagine an airplane racing down the runway. You hear the rumbling noise of the wheels on the ground, but this wheel noise stops as soon as the plane leaves the ground. Concentrate on the ideas, and the sound will stop when your reading takes off.

When you're ready, begin reading the first thousand words of

The Life and Adventures of Robinson Crusoe by Daniel Defoe

145

The Life and Adventures of Robinson Crusoe

I was born in the year 1632, in the city of York, of a good family, though not of that country, my father being a foreigner of Bremen, who settled first at Hull: he got a good estate by merchandise, and leaving off his trade, lived afterwards at York, from whence he had married my mother, whose relations were named Robinson, a very good family in that country, and from whom I was called Robinson Kreutznaer; but by the usual corruption of words in England, we are now called, nay we call ourselves, and write our name Crusoe, and so my companions always called me.

I had two elder brothers, one of which was lieutenant-colonel to an English regiment of foot in Flanders, formerly commanded by the famous Colonel Lockhart, and was killed at the battle near Dunkirk against the Spaniards. What became of my second brother I never knew, any more than my father or mother did know what was become of me.

Being the third son of the family, and not bred to any trade, my head began to be filled very early with rambling thoughts: my father, who was very ancient, had given me a competent share of learning, as far as house education and a country free-school generally go, and designed me for the law; but I would be satisfied with nothing but going to sea; and my inclination to this led me so strongly against the will, nay the commands of my father, and against all the entreaties and persuasions of my mother and other friends, that there seemed to be something fatal in that propension of nature tending directly to the life of misery which was to befall me.

My father, a wise and grave man, gave me serious and excellent counsel against what he foresaw was my design. He called me one morning into his chamber, where he was confined by the gout, and expostulated very warmly with me upon this subject: he asked me what reasons more than a mere wandering inclination I had for leaving my father's house and my native country, where I might be well introduced, and had a prospect of raising my fortune by application and industry, with a life of ease and pleasure. He told me it was for men of desperate fortunes on one hand, or of aspiring superior fortunes on the other, who went abroad upon adventures, to rise by enterprise, and make themselves famous in undertakings of a nature out of the common road; that these things were all either too far above me, or too far below me; that mine was the middle state, or what might be called the upper station of low life, which he had found by long experience was the best state in the world, the most suited to human happiness, not exposed to the miseries and hardships, the labor and sufferings of the mechanic part of mankind, and not embarrassed with the pride, luxury, ambition, and envy of the upper part of mankind, he told me, I might judge of the happiness of this state by this one thing, viz. that this was the state of life which all other people envied; that kings have frequently lamented the miserable consequences of being born to great things, and wish they had been placed in the middle of the two extremes, between the mean and the great; that the wise man gave his testimony to this as the just standard of true felicity, when he prayed to have neither poverty nor riches.

He bid me observe it, and I should always find, that the calamities of life were shared among the upper and lower part of mankind; but that the middle station had the fewest disasters, and was not exposed to so many vicissitudes as the higher or lower part of mankind; nay, they were not subjected to so many distempers and uneasinesses, either of body or mind, as those were, who by vicious living, luxury, and extravagances, on one hand, or by hard labor, want of necessaries, and mean or insufficient diet, on the other hand, bring distempers upon themselves by the natural consequences of their way of living; that the middle station of life was calculated for all kind of virtues and all kind of enjoyments; that peace and plenty were the handmaids of a middle fortune; that temperance, moderation, quietness, health, society, all agreeable diversions, and all desirable pleasures, were the blessings attending the middle station of life; that this way men went silently and smoothly through the world, and comfortably out of it, not embarrassed with the labors of the hands or of the head, not sold to the life of slavery for daily bread, or harassed with perplexed circumstances, which rob the soul of peace, and the body of rest; not enraged with the passion of envy, or secret burning lust of ambition for great things; but in easy circumstances sliding gently through the world, and sensibly tasting the sweets of living, without the bitter, feeling that they are happy, and learning by every day's experience to know it more sensibly.

After this, he pressed me earnestly, and in the most affectionate manner, not to play the young man, not to precipitate myself into miseries which nature and the station of life I was born in seemed to have provided against; that I was under no necessity of seeking my bread; that he would do well for me, and endeavor to enter me fairly into the station of life which he had been just recommending to me; and that if I was not very easy and happy in the world, it must be my mere fate or fault that must hinder it, and that he should have nothing to answer for, having thus discharged his duty in warning me against measures which he knew would be to my hurt: in a word, that as he would do very kind things for me if...

Chapter 13: Visualizing

The Key

It's not possible to think of two things at the same time. You can't concentrate on *how* you are reading, while also concentrating on *what* you are reading.

The recommended techniques discussed so far may seem obvious, maybe even platitudinous. Sure, it would be helpful if we read groups of words at a time and yes, better comprehension could avoid verbalizing and regression. And few would disagree with trying to conceptualize or see the big picture and true meaning of what you read. But you can't possibly think of all these things while also thinking about *what* you are reading.

The key to these reading techniques is *visualizing*.

Visualizing is not just one of the techniques—it is the *key* to engaging these other techniques while you are reading. Visualizing doesn't interfere with thinking about what you are reading, because it *IS* thinking about what you are reading. Visualizing is just thinking about it with your right brain, the parallel-processing hemisphere that has its own very effective way of rapidly understanding large amounts of information.

Whenever you try to visualize information, you are asking your right brain to take a look at it. This is the reason that visualizing is the key to the other techniques; it leads your right brain to automatically do the following:

1. **Conceptualize** ideas.
2. See the **big picture.**
3. Read in **phrases.**
4. Recognize the real **meaning.**
5. Read in **silence.**
6. Move **forward** without regression.
7. **Filter** out internal and external distractions.
8. Notice **connections** between new and existing knowledge.

9. Save information in the long-term *memory.*
10. *Comprehend* faster.
11. Increase *reading speed.*

Visualizing is actually a method of staying tuned in to and making stronger connections to your reading. Visualizing is not always easy—nor is it always perfect—but the more you visualize, the more the other effective habits will follow. Visualizing is what tips over the first domino as you start reading with the right brain.

Focusing on visualizing automatically involves the right brain, because this is the part of your brain that handles visualizing. It sees pictures as whole ideas, not just strings of information like your left brain does. These big-picture ideas are the larger, more meaningful representations of information.

Visualizing with the right brain is when the real "mind-meld" takes place, linking your mind to the author's. It's when you *see* the author's thoughts. The information that started as a concept in the author's mind now becomes a concept in yours.

Types of Visualizing

Words, letters, spelling, and phonics are simply communication tools. They are symbols and devices used to send ideas from one mind to another. Actual communication occurs only after ideas are transmitted, received and then finally connected to related ideas in the receiving mind.

Visualizing helps you move beyond communication symbols to concentrating on the actual *content* of the communications. To visualize the content, you must concentrate on meaning.

This does not mean stopping to mentally draw a beautifully detailed image of the meaning of each idea. Instead, think more in terms of rapid movie frames flashing through your mind, each idea going by in an instant. Some are simple; some are vague. Some are clear; some are complex. Some may be mere ghosts of an idea, and some may be realistic. And some may not be images at all.

You can easily imagine a picture of an *object*, but what about ideas you can't imagine as a picture? What about abstract ideas?

There are two ways to handle abstract ideas:

1. Metaphorical Visualizing
2. Conceptual Visualizing

Some ideas, although abstract, can sometimes be visualized as images metaphorically. An example would be imagining a heart to represent an abstract phrase like *"fell in love."*

But visualizing can also mean simply imagining the idea itself— that is, visualizing its *concept*. In this case, you wouldn't see any real picture at all, but instead just imagine the *meaning*. Rather than seeing images, this type of visualizing would be more like what you do when you say, "I *see* what you mean."

An image is only one part of a concept. Some concepts can include both pictorial and abstract information, while others can be completely abstract with no pictorial images at all. For these abstract ideas, you would be *visualizing concepts*.

Visualizing Concepts

To understand visualizing concepts, you first need to be clear what is meant by concepts and what is meant by visualizing.

Here are some dictionary definitions of concept:

1. A *general* notion or idea.
2. An idea of something formed mentally combining all its *characteristics* or particulars.
3. A directly conceived or intuited object of *thought*.

So you could combine these definitions to say a concept is a *general* idea—formed by combining all its *characteristics*—into an object of *thought*.

To conceptualize something is to mentally combine all of its characteristics. These characteristics are the attributes of the idea, its distinguishing traits, qualities, and properties. Considered together, these attributes represent the *essence* of the thing or idea.

For example, the concept of the word "dog" is a mental model including all the things that make something doggish. To conceptualize "dog," you could imagine something with the attributes of fur, four legs, and a tail.

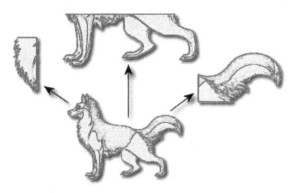

But concepts are not limited to physical attributes. Your concept of "dog" could also include canine behaviors and dogs you've known, as well as what you think of dogs. Basically, the concept of "dog" is everything "dog" means to you. And your concept of "dog," although probably similar to the concept held by most people, is uniquely your own; it is based on your very own life experiences and ideas.

So when you read "dog," you can instantly imagine your *concept* of a dog. Since a dog is a physical thing, your concept might also still include an actual image of a dog.

But what about the concept of "pet"? The concept of "pet" is more abstract than "dog." There are many types of pets, so which pet should you picture? You could select an arbitrary pet to imagine, or else a group of many types of pets together, but the real concept of "pet" is actually *any* pet, not one or a group.

To visualize the concept of "pet," you would need to imagine something pet-like, a generic, non-descript concept which includes all the attributes—friendly, docile, loyal, etc.—that make something pet-like to you.

But it will be difficult to create a real mental picture of "pet." This is how conceptualizing an abstract idea is different than merely visualizing a mental picture. For the more abstract concepts, you don't *picture* the idea, because there is no picture; instead, you imagine all the attributes that, in your mind, contribute to the concept.

Now for one step further into abstraction. How would you conceptualize "friendly"? The idea of "dog" might at least have a generic image, and "pet" may possibly have too many images, but "friendly" has no physical image at all. You can't draw a picture of "friendly," but you can still imagine all the attributes (helpful, trusting, pleasant, etc.) common to all the other "friendly" things you know.

What you are doing is considering the essence of what things are, whether this includes physical attributes or abstract. That's why considering the essence of ideas is more than just a reading technique, but a way of thinking. Visualizing what you read is thinking *conceptually*. This type of thinking is what lifts your reading to another level—to right brain reading.

What's in a Name?

Now that we've put physical images in their place as just one type of attribute, what about the *name* attribute?

The name attribute is the actual word or words used to describe the information, such as the words "dog," "pet," or "friendly." The name is one attribute of the concept, but it is not even necessary for conceptual understanding. In fact, it's quite possible to conceptualize something before you even know what it is called.

Here's a food I'd never seen until recently.

I didn't know its name, but I could still conceptualize it as a food, a plant, probably a fruit, and as something very strange looking to me.

It could have had a sign over it, describing it like this:

佛手柑

After seeing this sign, the next time I wanted to find one of these items, I could look for it by "name" by looking for this sign. But I would be "reading" the sign without saying the word, because I wouldn't know the sound of the word since I don't know Chinese.

The point here is that it is possible to read and understand words without thinking of the words or their sounds. I could simply *look* at this "word" and this would lead me to conceptualize this food.

I wouldn't have to know that this was pronounced *fat-sau-gam* in order to conceptualize the meaning of the word. But even knowing one of the English names—fingered citron, Buddha's hand, or bergamot—would really add nothing to my understanding. No matter what the name is, the idea—the concept—would still be the same, and the name would still be irrelevant.

The same goes for more familiar items. This could be described as

苹

or as **"apple."** Either name, written or verbal, is still just a symbol. You could conceptualize this item as a group of several attributes, such as taste, shape, color, food group, texture, and *name*, but the name is just one attribute—one that is only required for communication, not conceptual understanding.

An apple by any other name—or no name at all—is still an apple.

Visually imagining ideas as you read, involves using faster and broader information pathways. Complex information processing is the most special of all human talents. As primarily visual animals, visualizing ideas is simply applying our special mental talents to the important task of information processing.

Visualizing is more than just a reading trick. You could consider it the foundation of speed reading. To read faster than speech, you need to switch to reading ideas, whether physical or metaphorical images, or abstract concepts.

Visualizing creates a strong mental conduit between the text and our conscious mind by adapting the information to the type of brain we have—a powerful, visual, pattern recognizing machine. The act of visualizing also forces us to pay more attention to our reading; thinking of the ideas rather than just "listening" to ourselves read the words. Visualizing forces us to form a conceptual idea of the information and ask the important question of, "What does this *mean* to me?"

Visualizing harnesses the full range of the cortical skills of your right brain: the imagery, the conceptualizing, the big-picture and essence of information, and all the instant connections those larger ideas initiate in your mind. This type of massive parallel processing is what allows your mind to move more information at a time. A mental picture truly is worth a thousand mental words.

Practice Exercise #13

Ready for another exercise? Then tip that first domino by focusing your attention on visualizing what you are reading. You can see pictures or simply imagine ideas, but get that right brain involved and forget about the words and sounds. Each phrase has a meaningful idea behind it; look at this idea. Your high-speed right brain will then begin to quickly process information in these larger, unified units of meaning.

And remember that you only want to see the *ideas*. The words are only the silent messengers transferring those ideas to your brain. When you look at a meaningful word-group and see what it means, skip the words and sounds. Quickly imagine the idea and move on.

When you're ready, begin reading the first thousand words of

Gulliver's Travels by Jonathan Swift

Gulliver's Travels

My father had a small estate in Nottinghamshire: I was the third of five sons. He sent me to Emanuel College in Cambridge at fourteen years old, where I resided three years, and applied myself close to my studies; but the charge of maintaining me, although I had a very scanty allowance, being too great for a narrow fortune, I was bound apprentice to Mr. James Bates, an eminent surgeon in London, with whom I continued four years. My father now and then sending me small sums of money, I laid them out in learning navigation, and other parts of the mathematics, useful to those who intend to travel, as I always believed it would be, sometime or other, my fortune to do. When I left Mr. Bates, I went down to my father: where, by the assistance of him and my uncle John, and some other relations, I got forty pounds, and a promise of thirty pounds a year to maintain me at Leyden: there I studied physic two years and seven months, knowing it would be useful in long voyages.

Soon after my return from Leyden, I was recommended by my good master, Mr. Bates, to be surgeon to the Swallow, Captain Abraham Pannel, commander; with whom I continued three years and a half, making a voyage or two into the Levant, and some other parts. When I came back I resolved to settle in London; to which Mr. Bates, my master, encouraged me, and by him I was recommended to several patients. I took part of a small house in the Old Jewry; and being advised to alter my condition, I married Mrs. Mary Burton, second daughter to Mr. Edmund Burton, hosier, in Newgate-street, with whom I received four hundred pounds for a portion.

But my good master Bates dying in two years after, and I having few friends, my business began to fail; for my conscience would not suffer me to imitate the bad practice of too many among my brethren. Having therefore consulted with my wife, and some of my acquaintance, I determined to go again to sea. I was surgeon successively in two ships, and made several voyages, for six years, to the East and West Indies, by which I got some addition to my fortune. My hours of leisure I spent in reading the best authors, ancient and modern, being always provided with a good number of books; and when I was ashore, in observing the manners and dispositions of the people, as well as learning their language; wherein I had a great facility, by the strength of my memory.

The last of these voyages not proving very fortunate, I grew weary of the sea, and intended to stay at home with my wife and family. I removed from the Old Jewry to Fetter Lane, and from thence to Wapping, hoping to get business among the sailors; but it would not turn to account. After three years' expectation that things would mend, I accepted an advantageous offer from Captain William Prichard, master of the Antelope, who was making a voyage to the South Sea. We set sail from Bristol, May 4, 1699, and our voyage was at first very prosperous.

It would not be proper, for some reasons, to trouble the reader with the particulars of our adventures in those seas; let it suffice to inform him, that in our passage from thence to the East Indies, we were driven by a violent storm to the north-west of Van Diemen's Land. By an observation, we found ourselves in the latitude of 30 degrees 2 minutes south. Twelve of our crew were dead by immoderate labor and ill food; the rest were in a very weak condition.

On the 5th of November, which was the beginning of summer in those parts, the weather being very hazy, the seamen spied a rock within half a cable's length of the ship; but the wind was so strong, that we were driven directly upon it, and immediately split. Six of the crew, of whom I was one, having let down the boat into the sea, made a shift to get clear of the ship and the rock. We rowed, by my computation, about three leagues, till we were able to work no longer, being already spent with labor while we were in the ship.

We therefore trusted ourselves to the mercy of the waves, and in about half an hour the boat was overset by a sudden flurry from the north. What became of my companions in the boat, as well as of those who escaped on the rock, or were left in the vessel, I cannot tell; but conclude they were all lost.

For my own part, I swam as fortune directed me, and was pushed forward by wind and tide. I often let my legs drop, and could feel no bottom; but when I was almost gone, and able to struggle no longer, I found myself within my depth; and by this time the storm was much abated. The declivity was so small, that I walked near a mile before I got to the shore, which I conjectured was about eight o'clock in the evening.

I then advanced forward near half a mile, but could not discover any sign of houses or inhabitants; at least I was in so weak a condition, that I did not observe them. I was extremely tired, and with that, and the heat of the weather, and about half a pint of brandy that I drank as I left the ship, I found myself much inclined to sleep. I lay down on the grass, which was very short and soft, where I slept sounder than ever I remembered to have done in my life, and, as I reckoned, about nine hours; for when I awaked, it was just daylight. I attempted to rise, but was not able to stir: for, as I happened to lie on my back, I found my arms and legs were strongly fastened on each side to the ground; and my hair, which was long and thick, tied down in the same manner. I likewise felt several slender ligatures across my body, from my armpits to my thighs...

Chapter 14: Conceptualizing

Conceptual Thinking

Not only are words—written or verbal—irrelevant after they are used to communicate, but words can actually interfere with conceptual understanding. Sometimes we mentally replace the real idea with its symbol or name. This is not thinking, but simply memorizing. Memorizing is not conceptualizing, but the more primitive *perceptualizing*—the kind of thinking animals do, and the kind of thinking we do as children. Memorizing is an important skill, but just collecting facts won't make you any smarter than inanimate objects such as books or computers.

Sometimes it seems like we wouldn't be able think if it weren't for words. When we think about thinking, we generally think about self-talk. For this reason, the power of conceptual thinking is often overlooked, and people frequently mistake thinking with speaking. But it is just as possible to think without speaking, as it is to speak without thinking.

The right brain may be silent, but it is actually where the higher order cognitions of conceptualizing and pattern recognition take place. It does not have verbal abilities, so we don't get to hear what it's doing, but this also means it is not confused by communication symbols.

As an example of conceptual versus perceptual thinking, here is how I taught my son Jason his numbers. Instead of showing him the symbols 1, 2, 3, 4, 5, 6, 7, 8, 9, 10, I made up flash cards that looked kind of like dominoes, and each number was represented by a distinct pattern of dots like this:

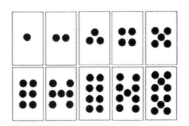

So, instead of thinking **2 + 3 = 5**, he would think:

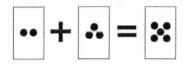

The result was that all his later arithmetic lessons made more sense to him; he was thinking of the concept of numbers rather than their memorized perceptual names. By learning his numbers conceptually rather than perceptually, he was able to quickly learn to add up strings of three-digit numbers in his head before he even started kindergarten. I'm embarrassed to sound like I am bragging here, but this is one of the best examples I can think of to demonstrate the power of conceptual thinking.

As you can tell, conceptual thinking goes beyond reading. Even when listening to someone speaking, you will find that you can listen more deeply if you conceptualize the things being said. With practice, you will get into the habit of noticing and appreciating real concepts during all types of communication.

I hope I don't appear to be overdoing this idea of conceptualizing, but the understanding of concepts is very important, and if it is unclear, the rest of this method could be difficult to follow. It's either going to sound like I'm only stating the obvious, that you should simply "think about" what you are reading, or it's just not going to work for you, and you won't know why.

Conceptual Reading

Hopefully all this is somewhat interesting to you, but I'm sure this might also seem like a lot to think about while trying to read. However, all of this is just background, an attempt to be sure we are talking about the same thing. While actually reading, you are only going to get quick flashes in your mind of what each concept is.

The important point is that these are going to be flashes of what the ideas mean to you, rather than just listening to what the words sound like. You might be surprised at how much information you can pass to your mind in an instant when your right brain is conceptualizing information as whole ideas.

For example, when you read the word "elephant," a lot of information moves from your eyes, through the various parts of your mind, and on to the many areas of your brain representing all the things this word means to you; and all of this happens virtually instantaneously. It sounds impossible, but so does the act of reaching your hand out to accurately intercept the trajectory of a ball without consciously performing any differential calculus. You don't have to completely understand how visualizing concepts works; you just need to recognize that it does work and how to take advantage of it.

Not only does conceptualizing create more meaningful connections to information, but simply the fact that you are paying more attention increases comprehension. So regardless of how many or how few attributes you associate with a concept, just applying this type of concentration—conceptual concentration—will make a big difference in the level of comprehension you experience. This is because the act of trying to visualize forces you to remain more involved with the material, and encourages you to think more about what you are reading. The ideas you read will become more real, will make more mental connections, and these connections will be made quicker and stronger than they would be from decoding the mere sound of words.

Conceptual Practice

As you practice, you will need to apply your imagination in order to visualize ideas. This means you may have to go slower at first, glancing at a phrase and then thinking of an image of the idea. If you read, "The man," you might picture a man. Then if you read, "lived in a house," you may picture the man in his house. And if you next read, "in the Northeast," you might picture the house in the top-right corner of a map.

The first two images would be physical images and the third a metaphorical representation. Anything will do, but just try to quickly visualize the meaning.

If no good images instantly come to mind, then conceptualize the idea— that is, think about what it means to you. For example, "for a long time" is more of an abstract idea, but you would conceptualize what this means to you; it could mean consistency, waiting, many years, or a large part of your life. Or, instead of an abstract concept, it could also be a metaphor, such as the image of a calendar. Everyone will do this differently because ideas mean slightly different things to each person. The only important thing is to practice actively thinking and imagining the meaning of what you are reading.

This may seem difficult at first. Reading with the right brain is almost like learning to write with your other hand. The left brain will always be where the text is converted into words, and it will take practice to develop the habit of passing this data to the right side, to recognize whole phrases as complete conceptual ideas.

But practice will make this skill quick and automatic, and the task of visualizing will no longer compete so much for mental resources. Until you reach that point, however, it will take more energy to visualize an idea than to simply continue to decipher words into sounds and definitions. For that reason, you may have to slow down at first while you learn to see the ideas.

Like any skill, someone can show you how, but you still have to do it yourself. Instruction is nothing without *construction*. Someone can give you instruction, but only you can complete the construction. Although proper instruction is important, you need to supply the practice. For example, simply reading about how to swim wouldn't prevent you from drowning. You have to jump in and practice on your own to form new habits. But once conceptualizing does becomes a habit, the ideas will seem to float off the page directly into your consciousness.

Learn to swim, and then swim.
-John Lennon when asked, "What's the meaning of life?"

Practice Exercise #14

Read the next practice exercise with your attention on the conceptual meaning of each phrase. Think about its real essence. Look *through* the words at the meaning *behind* them. Allow this to slow you down at first if necessary, but make sure to imagine the ideas and then allow this clearer comprehension to lift your reading speed. Conceptualize ideas and read with your whole mind.

When you're ready, begin reading the first thousand words of

***Twenty Thousand Leagues Under the Sea* by Jules Verne**

Twenty Thousand Leagues Under the Sea

The year 1866 was signalized by a remarkable incident, a mysterious and puzzling phenomenon, which doubtless no one has yet forgotten. Not to mention rumors which agitated the maritime population and excited the public mind, even in the interior of continents, seafaring men were particularly excited. Merchants, common sailors, captains of vessels, skippers, both of Europe and America, naval officers of all countries, and the Governments of several States on the two continents, were deeply interested in the matter.

For some time past vessels had been met by "an enormous thing," a long object, spindle-shaped, occasionally phosphorescent, and infinitely larger and more rapid in its movements than a whale.

The facts relating to this apparition (entered in various log-books) agreed in most respects as to the shape of the object or creature in question, the untiring rapidity of its movements, its surprising power of locomotion, and the peculiar life with which it seemed endowed. If it was a whale, it surpassed in size all those hitherto classified in science. Taking into consideration the mean of observations made at divers' times—rejecting the timid estimate of those who assigned to this object a length of two hundred feet, equally with the exaggerated opinions which set it down as a mile in width and three in length—we might fairly conclude that this mysterious being surpassed greatly all dimensions admitted by the learned ones of the day, if it existed at all. And that it DID exist was an undeniable fact; and, with that tendency which disposes the human mind in favor of the marvelous, we can understand the excitement produced in the entire world by this supernatural apparition. As to classing it in the list of fables, the idea was out of the question.

On the 20th of July, 1866, the steamer Governor Higginson, of the Calcutta and Burnach Steam Navigation Company, had met this moving mass five miles off the east coast of Australia. Captain Baker thought at first that he was in the presence of an unknown sandbank; he even prepared to determine its exact position when two columns of water, projected by the mysterious object, shot with a hissing noise a hundred and fifty feet up into the air. Now, unless the sandbank had been submitted to the intermittent eruption of a geyser, the Governor

Higginson had to do neither more nor less than with an aquatic mammal, unknown till then, which threw up from its blow-holes columns of water mixed with air and vapor.

Similar facts were observed on the 23rd of July in the same year, in the Pacific Ocean, by the Columbus, of the West India and Pacific Steam Navigation Company. But this extraordinary creature could transport itself from one place to another with surprising velocity; as, in an interval of three days, the Governor Higginson and the Columbus had observed it at two different points of the chart, separated by a distance of more than seven hundred nautical leagues.

Fifteen days later, two thousand miles farther off, the Helvetia, of the Compagnie-Nationale, and the Shannon, of the Royal Mail Steamship Company, sailing to windward in that portion of the Atlantic lying between the United States and Europe, respectively signaled the monster to each other in 42° 15' N. latitude and 60° 35' W. longitude. In these simultaneous observations they thought themselves justified in estimating the minimum length of the mammal at more than three hundred and fifty feet, as the Shannon and Helvetia were of smaller dimensions than it, though they measured three hundred feet over all.

Now the largest whales, those which frequent those parts of the sea round the Aleutian, Kulammak, and Umgullich Islands, have never exceeded the length of sixty yards, if they attain that.

In every place of great resort, the monster was the fashion. They sang of it in the cafes, ridiculed it in the papers, and represented it on the stage. All kinds of stories were circulated regarding it. There appeared in the papers caricatures of every gigantic and imaginary creature, from the white whale, the terrible "Moby Dick" of sub-arctic regions, to the immense kraken, whose tentacles could entangle a ship of five hundred tons and hurry it into the abyss of the ocean. The legends of ancient times were even revived.

Then burst forth the unending argument between the believers and the unbelievers in the societies of the wise and the scientific journals. "The question of the monster" inflamed all minds. Editors of scientific journals, quarrelling with believers in the supernatural, spilled seas of ink during this memorable campaign, some even drawing blood; for from the sea-serpent they came to direct personalities.

During the first months of the year 1867 the question seemed buried, never to revive, when new facts were brought before the public. It was then no longer a scientific problem to be solved, but a real danger seriously to be avoided. The question took quite another shape. The monster became a small island, a rock, a reef, but a reef of indefinite and shifting proportions.

On the 5th of March, 1867, the Moravian, of the Montreal Ocean Company, finding herself during the night in 27° 30' latitude and 72° 15' longitude, struck on her starboard quarter a rock, marked in no chart for that part of the sea. Under the combined efforts of the wind and its four hundred horse power, it was going at the rate of thirteen knots. Had it not been for the superior strength of the hull of the Moravian, she would have been broken...

Chapter 15: Reading Speeds

Averages

What reading speed would you like to achieve?

Although the average reading speed is two hundred fifty words per minute, more than half of the people read below that speed. If it seems like a discrepancy that more than half read below average, it's only because those very rare, really fast readers are pulling up the overall average of everyone else.

For example, if in a group of eight people, seven people read at 200 WPM and one person reads at 600 WPM, then the average for all eight people would be 250 WPM, because (200 x 7 + 600) / 8 = 250. So in this example, even though the average is two hundred fifty, most people are still reading below average, at only two hundred words per minute.

The chart below gives you an approximate idea of the distribution of adult reading speeds.

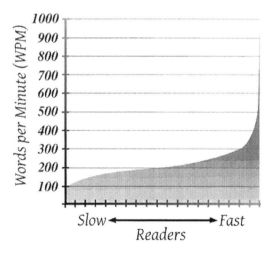

As you can see, half the readers (the left half of the chart) are reading below two hundred words per minute. And although there is a gradual increase in faster readers to the right, there are only a very few who are reading above four hundred words per minute, fewer still who read above six hundred (the generally accepted "speed reading" level), and an absolutely microscopic number of people who reach one thousand words per minute.

For college students, the average speed is slightly higher at three hundred words per minute, with most students reading between two hundred and four hundred words per minute. But only one in twenty college students reads faster than four hundred words per minute.

Of course we're talking here about *real* reading, reading for content and comprehension. Other types of text consumption and their associated average college-level speeds are below:

- Scanning: 600 WPM
- Skimming: 450 WPM
- Reading: 300 WPM
- Learning: 200 WPM
- Memorizing: 130 WPM

In fact, for real reading, the upper limits are usually much lower than most people are aware (especially compared to the inflated claims of many "speed reading" courses).

Ronald Carver, author of the 1990 book *The Causes of High and Low Reading Achievement*, has done extensive testing of readers and reading speeds, thoroughly examining the various speed reading techniques and actual improvements likely to be gained. One test he completed pitted four groups of the fastest readers he could find against each other. The groups consisted of champion speed readers, fast college readers, successful professionals whose jobs required a lot of reading, and students who had scored highest on speed reading tests. Carver found that of his superstars, none could read faster than six hundred words per minute with more than a seventy-five percent retention rate.

Even though the claims of most speed reading courses offer more hype than hope, there is still plenty of room for honest and impressive improvement. For most people, this means they are very possibly able to double or triple their reading speed. If your reading rate falls in the middle of the average reading speeds, and you double your speed from two hundred to four hundred words per minute, this could be life-changing, because reading quickly is a very different experience than reading slowly. Faster reading is much more interesting, more memorable, and less frustrating.

And just consider the time savings. If someone who read two hundred words per minute picked up an average novel of eighty thousand words, it would take that person six hours and forty minutes of reading time to reach the end of the novel—that's spending most of a whole day reading. But at four hundred words per minute, it would only take three hours and twenty minutes to finish that same book, leaving the rest of the day free for anything else.

What if you didn't want to finish the book in one sitting, though? How about reading one chapter? Assuming an average page of three hundred words and an average chapter of twenty pages, the chapter would take either a half an hour or fifteen minutes if you read two hundred or four hundred words per minute. Or you could look at it is the difference between reading forty pages per hour versus eighty pages per hour.

OK, that's a lot of numbers, but hopefully they give you an idea of what even a modest speed increase can do for you. If you think about the ability to read eighty pages per hour, you will realize that you will read more, not just because you are saving time, but because a lot more reading will be worth your effort with that lower time requirement.

Also, note that all of these figures are average numbers. Average people are not reading phrases. Most fast reading is done simply by pushing the reading speeds, basically applying brute force to the task. Reading phrases is about training your mind to read in your imagination instead of in your ears, learning to use a different part of your brain and use it in a different way. But learning to do this takes a completely different way of looking at reading and a different way of thinking about the process. So even though the averages may be slower than many people realize, using a different approach to reading will make it easier to reach the higher speeds of those rare speed readers.

But still, please remember that increased reading speed can only come as a result of faster comprehension. If you forget this, you will concentrate on the wrong thing. To learn to read faster, you must learn to comprehend faster.

Flexibility

As mentioned in chapter nine, conceptual processing is the part of reading which takes the most time. This is the weakest link in reading and is also where the largest variations in speed occur.

Most of this speed variation is due to the difficulty of—or your preexisting knowledge about—the material. A useful analogy is to imagine riding a bicycle over a changing terrain.

If you were riding over a nice, smooth, level, and familiar terrain, you could switch into a higher gear and ride much faster. Similar to this, when you are reading easy or more familiar text, you can take in larger word-groups at a time and at higher speeds.

When you encounter harder or unfamiliar material, you need to automatically slow down and also read shorter word-groups, just as you would switch to a lower gear and cover less distance with each rotation of your bicycle pedal.

Writing style can also slow you down. A text that is strangely worded or full of unusual words may require you to slow way down, as you would when riding on an uneven or bumpy road.

And then there are the occasional unknown words or even grammatical errors where you must slow down and be even more careful, like riding over an old rutted dirt road.

In fact, there are many reading situations which will constantly impact your speed:

- Lists
- Names
- Dialogue
- Narration
- New words
- Convoluted sentences
- Spelling or grammar errors
- Passive versus active sentences
- Beginnings of sentences, paragraphs, and chapters

You can never read at a constant static speed and expect your comprehension to adjust. Instead you must let comprehension take the lead, and allow your speed to adjust.

Contextual Reading

One tip that will help you find your comprehension speed is to make sure you have a firm grasp on what you are reading as you get started. Regardless of the reading terrain, you should always start off slow, in first gear. This gives you time to get your balance and to establish traction while you get a firm grip on the subject and context of what you are reading.

Starting off slowly is helpful, but it can also be awfully hard to remember because we can be so anxious to read fast that we kind of forget *why* we are reading (to understand the text, right?). But each time you start reading, you usually need to go slow for a bit until you pick up the thread of the ideas. This can also be useful, to a lesser degree, at the beginning of paragraphs and sentences.

So, if you concentrate on the ideas and not on your speed, you will find your speed will increase when it's ready. Of course, concentration on visualization and conceptualization will go a long way to automatically accommodate these changes; the information itself determines the time it takes for you to visualize and conceptualize and will therefore automatically control your reading speed.

By allowing yourself time to make a connection with your reading, you will start to "see" the ideas and your reading will begin to flow. Forcing the speed too quickly will only leave you skimming over the material without comprehension. This can be a difficult habit to overcome, because you will want to push your speed, but you have to get connected, and stay connected, to the material before you can read fast.

Maintaining this contextual connection while reading can have a major effect on what the text means to you. For example, look at how the first phrase changes your perception of the second in these two combinations:

1. Wash dishes. Polish silverware.
2. German dishes. Polish silverware.

"Polish silverware" means something quite different in example two than it does in example one. This is why taking a little more time when you first start to read will give you a strong enough context to better anticipate the proper meaning.

Thinking Ahead

Similar to contextual reading; is anticipatory reading. Anticipatory reading lets you get in sync with the material to more easily anticipate upcoming phrases. When you do this, you can fly past those anticipated phrases as you merely need to verify your predictions.

This also makes your reading smoother. Thinking ahead while you are reading is like looking farther down the road instead of at the pavement right in front of you. This makes it much easier to go faster as there are fewer course corrections necessary; comprehension is increased due to the contextual clues of the preceding text.

Thinking ahead and anticipating what the text will say will also help you stay in the zone by avoiding surprises. Like when you ride a bicycle, you're a lot less wobbly when you look ahead rather than down at the ground beneath you.

Anticipatory reading is reading aggressively, looking ahead and anticipating where the author is going. Everything you read will therefore be more firmly attached to what has gone before and what lies ahead.

Speed Minimums

Although comprehension will determine your speed, it is a good idea to try still to maintain a certain minimum speed if possible. Just as riding a bike too slowly can make it difficult to maintain your balance, reading too slowly makes it difficult to take in larger ideas at a time and to avoid slipping into the old habit of verbalizing.

Of course, it will still be necessary to read very slowly at times, but unless the situation demands it, a slightly faster speed will usually be helpful. You don't want to read faster than your comprehension, but reading fast enough can also *help* comprehension by maintaining your reading momentum. It's a balancing act, and sometimes you will even lose your balance, but just be flexible and do your best.

Another way to apply the bicycle analogy is by comparing the black and gray text used in this book to training wheels. It is a tool which helps you by removing one of the tasks—balancing the bike or finding the phrases— while you practice and get comfortable with the rest of the skills you need to acquire—pedaling and steering, or reading whole ideas and visualizing. You are supported by black and gray "thought-units."

I hope I didn't stretch this analogy too far, but analogies can be very powerful aids to understanding concepts. In fact, analogies are actually quite conceptual in their very nature because they work by attaching new ideas to familiar ones via the attributes they have in common.

But no matter how fast or slow you read, *any* speed is better than reading without comprehension. As much as you would love to read faster and no matter what your current capabilities are, there is no reading at all if you do not understand what you read. So even if you think reading conceptually is slowing you down at first, it may be that your old "faster" speed wasn't really reading at all, but merely recognizing the words.

Everyone learning to improve their reading, starts at a different place and with different strengths and weaknesses. Since this book is designed to help people read better, the more help you need, the more help this book will be able to offer. Some people will make more gains than others, and no one really knows what their potential is until they reach it. But all practice is good and never a waste of time. The only wasted time is the time wasted before deciding to start improving your reading.

Practice Exercise #15

As your read the next practice exercise, remember that speed will only come from more powerful comprehension. Read for the ideas; if you visualize it, the speed will come.

The two main things to remember about reading faster are to concentrate on comprehension, and be flexible. Speed will be the reward of this comprehension and flexibility.

When you're ready, begin reading the first thousand words of

The Three Musketeers by Alexandre Dumas

The Three Musketeers

On the first Monday of the month of April, 1625, the market town of Meung, in which the author of ROMANCE OF THE ROSE was born, appeared to be in as perfect a state of revolution as if the Huguenots had just made a second La Rochelle of it. Many citizens, seeing the women flying toward the High Street, leaving their children crying at the open doors, hastened to don the cuirass, and supporting their somewhat uncertain courage with a musket or a partisan, directed their steps toward the hostelry of the Jolly Miller, before which was gathered, increasing every minute, a compact group, vociferous and full of curiosity.

In those times panics were common, and few days passed without some city or other registering in its archives an event of this kind. There were nobles, who made war against each other; there was the king, who made war against the cardinal; there was Spain, which made war against the king. Then, in addition to these concealed or public, secret or open wars, there were robbers, mendicants, Huguenots, wolves, and scoundrels, who made war upon everybody. The citizens always took up arms readily against thieves, wolves or scoundrels, often against nobles or Huguenots, sometimes against the king, but never against cardinal or Spain. It resulted, then, from this habit that on the said first Monday of April, 1625, the citizens, on hearing the clamor, and seeing neither the red-and-yellow standard nor the livery of the Duc de Richelieu, rushed toward the hostel of the Jolly Miller. When arrived there, the cause of the hubbub was apparent to all.

A young man—we can sketch his portrait at a dash. Imagine to yourself a Don Quixote of eighteen; a Don Quixote without his corselet, without his coat of mail, without his cuisses; a Don Quixote clothed in a woolen doublet, the blue color of which had faded into a nameless shade between lees of wine and a heavenly azure; face long and brown; high cheek bones, a sign of sagacity; the maxillary muscles enormously developed, an infallible sign by which a Gascon may always be detected, even without his cap—and our young man wore a cap set off with a sort of feather; the eye open and intelligent; the nose hooked, but finely chiseled. Too big for a youth, too small for a grown man, an experienced eye might have taken him for a farmer's son upon a journey had it not been for the long sword which, dangling from a leather baldric, hit against the calves of its owner as he walked, and against the rough side of his steed when he was on horseback.

For our young man had a steed which was the observed of all observers. It was a Bearn pony, from twelve to fourteen years old, yellow in his hide, without a hair in his tail, but not without windgalls on his legs, which, though going with his head lower than his knees, rendering a martingale quite unnecessary, contrived nevertheless to perform his eight leagues a day. Unfortunately, the qualities of this horse were so well concealed under his strange-colored hide and his unaccountable gait, that at a time when everybody was a connoisseur in horseflesh, the appearance of the aforesaid pony at Meung—which place he had entered about a quarter of an hour before, by the gate of Beaugency—produced an unfavorable feeling, which extended to his rider.

And this feeling had been more painfully perceived by young d'Artagnan—for so was the Don Quixote of this second Rosinante named—from his not being able to conceal from himself the ridiculous appearance that such a steed gave him, good horseman as he was. He had sighed deeply, therefore, when accepting the gift of the pony from M. d'Artagnan the elder. He was not ignorant that such a beast was worth at least twenty livres; and the words which had accompanied the present were above all price.

"My son," said the old Gascon gentleman, in that pure Bearn PATOIS of which Henry IV could never rid himself, "this horse was born in the house of your father about thirteen years ago, and has remained in it ever since, which ought to make you love it. Never sell it; allow it to die tranquilly and honorably of old age, and if you make a campaign with it, take as much care of it as you would of an old servant. At court, provided you have ever the honor to go there," continued M. d'Artagnan the elder, "—an honor to which, remember, your ancient nobility gives you the right—sustain worthily your name of gentleman, which has been worthily borne by your ancestors for five hundred years, both for your own sake and the sake of those who belong to you. By the latter I mean your relatives and friends. Endure nothing from anyone except Monsieur the Cardinal and the king. It is by his courage, please observe, by his courage alone, that a gentleman can make his way nowadays. Whoever hesitates for a second perhaps allows the bait to escape which during that exact second fortune held out to him. You are young. You ought to be brave for two reasons: the first is that you are a Gascon, and the second is that you are my son. Never fear quarrels, but seek adventures. I have taught you how to handle a sword; you have thews of iron, a wrist of steel. Fight on all occasions. Fight the more for duels being forbidden, since consequently there is twice as much courage in fighting. I have nothing to give you, my son, but fifteen crowns, my horse, and the counsels you have just heard. Your mother will add to them a recipe for a certain balsam, which she had from a Bohemian and which has the miraculous virtue of curing all the wounds...

Chapter 16: Comprehension Speeds

Information Speed

Information speed is the speed at which information enters your mind. If this could be measured, it would be more meaningful than words per minute. In fact, words per minute is actually pretty meaningless without considering information speed.

Since real reading is comprehension, the speed of your real reading is the speed in which you are collecting information. Instead of words per minute (WPM), it would be more useful to think in terms of information per minute (IPM). IPM would be the speedometer that tells you how fast you are actually traveling, whereas WPM would be the tachometer that only tells you how fast your engine is spinning.

In other words, sometimes you would be reading at a high WPM over easy material, and at other times slowing down to a lower WPM to conceptualize a new idea. But your real IPM speed would actually be much more constant with a consistent flow of information per minute continually reaching your brain. The reason IPM is more stable is because it is generally determined by the speed your brain can process ideas.

But there is another factor which can affect WPM—language density. Not only does the amount of information in text vary, but the length of text needed to express this same information can also be longer or shorter.

An author can choose longer or shorter words to say roughly the same thing. He can use a "five dollar word rather than a fifty-cent word," as Mark Twain put it.

For example, an author could use the word "accomplish" when the word "do" would do, use the word "expenditure" for "cost," or use "fundamental" for "basic." When measuring pages per minute or standard word length per minute, it would seem that you were reading faster when longer words were used. However, you would really only be pedaling faster, not making any additional progress since your true information speed would be unchanged.

This is not to say whether longer or shorter words are better, since this depends on the author's style and vocabulary. This is only to demonstrate that information speed is quite separate from "reading" speed and that even when your words per minute rate slows down, you are not necessarily "reading" any slower.

Language Speed

Another indication that information speed is more constant than word speed is the impact that different languages have on speaking speed. Each language has its own natural speed. When you listen to some languages, people often sound as if they are speaking very fast. This is because most languages are less dense than English, which means they require more syllables to communicate the same ideas.

French researchers at Lyon University constructed an interesting comparison of language density. They measured the total length of time and number of syllables per second it takes people speaking different languages to express the same sentences translated into their own languages.

The research study found that the average Spanish speaker speaks twenty-five percent more syllables per second than the average English speaker. But the same translated sentences still took about the same overall time to speak in each language. The Spanish language used more syllables to say the same thing, but they still communicated roughly the same amount of information per minute.

If you've ever listened to someone speaking Spanish, you may have thought they were speaking faster than what you are accustomed to hearing in English. They are... but still they aren't *communicating* any faster.

For example, compare the following sentences in English and Spanish.

This is an example of text in English and Spanish. You can see how much longer Spanish is than English.

Este es un ejemplo de texto en Inglés y Español. Se puede ver cuánto tiempo más el español es de Inglés.

Each sentence says the same thing, and although the written sentences are similar in length (due to the strangeness of English spelling), the number of syllables is 30% longer in Spanish (35 syllables in Spanish vs. 27 in English). But each native speaker would still take about the same length of time to say the sentence.

Each language studied showed the same pattern—languages that used more syllables to express the same ideas were spoken at a higher rate of syllables per minute and higher density languages were spoken at a slower rate.

Two conclusions can be made from this:

1. Comprehension speed is more constant than language speed (IPM is more constant than WPM).
2. Comprehension determines speed—not only in reading but even in speech.

We apparently have a certain speed that we can comprehend information, and it's that speed limit which determines both how fast we speak and how fast we read. This is just more evidence that to read faster, you must comprehend faster.

Fiction vs. Non-Fiction

Here's a common lament: "Why would I want to read fiction faster? Wouldn't I want to read it slowly in order to savor it?" Or there's this: "How could I possibly read non-fiction faster? Wouldn't I need to go slow in order to understand or remember it?" From these two comments, it seems like you can only read fast, if the book is not fiction... and not non-fiction!

As to fiction, yes, you may want to read this slower if you wish to savor the sounds of the language. In this case, you are more interested in reading as a performance—like reading poetry. If, however, you are reading to enjoy a story, then it wouldn't make any more sense to read this story slowly than it would to "savor" a movie in slow-motion!

"But wait," I hear you saying, "I only want to read it at 'regular' speed!" Oh? Are you *sure* your current speed is *regular* and other speeds are not? There is no "right" speed. As long as you understand what you are reading, then you are reading at the right speed. It's the speed of thought, not the speed of the clock, which determines your comprehension speed.

For example, have you ever noticed that what might have seemed like a long dream when you were sleeping actually occurred over a very short time? This is because time is relative, and the faster you think, the slower time appears to be. When you were dreaming, you were thinking faster and the dream events were happening faster than in "real" time. This shows not only that the experience of time is relative, but also that you are actually capable of much faster thinking than you may have realized.

The truth is, you *can* enjoy a book at faster speeds. In fact, faster speeds are even more enjoyable in some ways. This is because when you get to the middle of the book, you will still remember the beginning, and the whole book will tie together better.

Now, non-fiction. Yes, it is very true that you must often slow down to read non-fiction. In fact, you often need to come to a complete stop while you consider something fascinating that you have never considered before. But this is not reading; this is pondering—a very enjoyable activity on its own, but a special side benefit of non-fiction. Stopping to consider something is not reading; it's more like sightseeing.

The one other step involved in reading non-fiction is the extra memory processing. If you are reading to learn something, then you need to do more than just understand it; you need to place it firmly in your memory where you can easily find it again. This is where information becomes knowledge. This step often takes time while you consider the different effects this new information has on your existing knowledge. What are all the connections and relationships to be considered? This too is not really a part of reading, but of organizing ideas after you read them and connecting them in new ways to create your own new ideas.

Not everything about non-fiction makes it slower to read though. There are some things about non-fiction which actually help you read faster. For one, non-fiction authors are often trying to convince you of something. This means an author will generally make a special effort to make his case logically and systematically, and extra effort put into the explanation can make it faster and easier to consume.

If you have the ability to read faster, you can always decide on your own what speed you prefer for fiction or non-fiction, but at least you will have the choice. The best reading speed is the fastest speed you can understand. There's no way to go faster and no need to go slower than comprehension speed.

Internal Factors

There are factors other than the material itself which will affect your comprehension speed, and these must also be accommodated. These are internal speed variations—things that are unique to you and your current situation.

Your own mental processing abilities will change based on things such as the time of day, your mood, or external and internal distractions. Although these factors come from within you, you don't really have much control over them except to recognize them and take them into account.

The best you can do is to be patient with yourself. You must allow yourself to be able to assimilate the information you read. If you are finding this difficult to do, then you must slow down. You almost have to be Zen-like in your reading, letting the information come to you. This does not mean reading words and just seeing what ideas come along. It means to visualize, and focus on conceptualizing, and let the text choose the speed. Relax and engage your imagination, forgetting about speed and immersing yourself in the information.

In my experience, this is the hardest part of reading faster—to stop concentrating on speed. It is natural to want to push your speed, and in fact this is what most speed reading courses recommend, that you push your speed as fast as you can. They even give you eye exercises to speed up your eyeballs, enabling them to bounce back and forth at maximum frequency.

But reading for ideas requires you to do the exact opposite; you must force yourself to slow down to the speed of comprehension and to make sure you have grasped a conceptual understanding of each piece of information before going to the next. Of course, this better grasp of the information will *lead* to faster reading, but in the meantime it can feel like you are forcing yourself to slow down. All you are really doing, however, is forcing yourself to remain connected to your real reading— your reading comprehension.

No matter how difficult it is to hold your reading speed to your comprehension speed, it is imperative that you let the speed come to you rather than chase after it. It's really a balancing act wherein on the one hand you have to be willing to let go of the words and move on as soon as you "get it," while on the other hand, not allow your speed to run away on you.

The takeaway is that to learn speed reading, you need to learn speed comprehension, because speed depends on comprehension and not vice versa. If you push your speed beyond your comprehension, it will be like Lucy and Ethel working at that chocolate-wrapping conveyer belt, with chocolates flying everywhere and very little getting wrapped.

Practice Exercise #16

As you read this next practice exercise, relax, be patient, and concentrate on imagining what you are reading. And instead of thinking about reading faster, just concentrate on meaning.

Also, remember to time your reading and record your words per minute in the chart you printed or in some other convenient place.

When you're ready, begin reading the first thousand words of

Moby Dick by Herman Melville

Moby Dick

Call me Ishmael. Some years ago—never mind how long precisely—having little or no money in my purse, and nothing particular to interest me on shore, I thought I would sail about a little and see the watery part of the world. It is a way I have of driving off the spleen and regulating the circulation. Whenever I find myself growing grim about the mouth; whenever it is a damp, drizzly November in my soul; whenever I find myself involuntarily pausing before coffin warehouses, and bringing up the rear of every funeral I meet; and especially whenever my hypos get such an upper hand of me, that it requires a strong moral principle to prevent me from deliberately stepping into the street, and methodically knocking people's hats off—then, I account it high time to get to sea as soon as I can. This is my substitute for pistol and ball. With a philosophical flourish Cato throws himself upon his sword; I quietly take to the ship. There is nothing surprising in this. If they but knew it, almost all men in their degree, sometime or other, cherish very nearly the same feelings towards the ocean with me.

There now is your insular city of the Manhattoes, belted round by wharves as Indian isles by coral reefs—commerce surrounds it with her surf. Right and left, the streets take you waterward. Its extreme downtown is the battery, where that noble mole is washed by waves, and cooled by breezes, which a few hours previous were out of sight of land. Look at the crowds of water-gazers there.

Circumambulate the city of a dreamy Sabbath afternoon. Go from Corlears Hook to Coenties Slip, and from thence, by Whitehall, northward. What do you see? Posted like silent sentinels all around the town, stand thousands upon thousands of mortal men fixed in ocean reveries. Some leaning against the spiles; some seated upon the pier-heads; some looking over the bulwarks of ships from China; some high aloft in the rigging, as if striving to get a still better seaward peep. But these are all landsmen; of week days pent up in lath and plaster—tied to counters, nailed to benches, clinched to desks. How then is this? Are the green fields gone? What do they here?

But look! Here come more crowds, pacing straight for the water, and seemingly bound for a dive. Strange! Nothing will content them but the extremest limit of the land; loitering under the shady lee of yonder warehouses will not suffice. No. They must get just as nigh the water as they possibly can without falling in. And there they stand—miles of them—leagues. Inlanders all, they come from lanes and alleys, streets and avenues—north, east, south, and west. Yet here they all unite. Tell me, does the magnetic virtue of the needles of the compasses of all those ships attract them thither?

Once more. Say you are in the country; in some high land of lakes. Take almost any path you please, and ten to one it carries you down in a dale, and leaves you there by a pool in the stream. There is magic in it. Let the most absent-minded of men be plunged in his deepest reveries—stand that man on his legs, set his feet a-going, and he will infallibly lead you to water, if water there be in all that region. Should you ever be athirst in the great American desert, try this experiment, if your caravan happens to be supplied with a metaphysical professor. Yes, as everyone knows, meditation and water are wedded forever.

But here is an artist. He desires to paint you the dreamiest, shadiest, quietest, most enchanting bit of romantic landscape in all the valley of the Saco. What is the chief element he employs? There stand his trees, each with a hollow trunk, as if a hermit and a crucifix were within; and here sleeps his meadow, and there sleep his cattle; and up from yonder cottage goes a sleepy smoke. Deep into distant woodlands winds a mazy way, reaching to overlapping spurs of mountains bathed in their hill-side blue. But though the picture lies thus tranced, and though this pine-tree shakes down its sighs like leaves upon this shepherd's head, yet all were vain, unless the shepherd's eye were fixed upon the magic stream before him. Go visit the Prairies in June, when for scores on scores of miles you wade knee-deep among Tiger-lilies—what is the one charm wanting? Water—there is not a drop of water there! Were Niagara but a cataract of sand, would you travel your thousand miles to see it? Why did the poor poet of Tennessee, upon suddenly receiving two handfuls of silver, deliberate whether to buy him a coat, which he sadly needed, or invest his money in a pedestrian trip to Rockaway Beach? Why is almost every robust healthy boy with a robust healthy soul in him, at some time or other crazy to go to sea? Why upon your first voyage as a passenger, did you yourself feel such a mystical vibration, when first told that you and your ship were now out of sight of land? Why did the old Persians hold the sea holy? Why did the

188

Greeks give it a separate deity, and own brother of Jove? Surely all this is not without meaning. And still deeper the meaning of that story of Narcissus, who because he could not grasp the tormenting, mild image he saw in the fountain, plunged into it and was drowned. But that same image, we ourselves see in all rivers and oceans. It is the image of the ungraspable phantom of life; and this is the key to it all.

Now, when I say that I am in the habit of going to sea whenever I begin to grow hazy about the eyes, and begin to be over conscious of my lungs, I do not mean to have it inferred that...

Chapter 17: Techniques

What techniques can keep your mind from slipping into its old reading habits and keep your attention on conceptualizing? Sometimes having the proper perspective of what you are doing will help.

Here is one analogy I find helpful in keeping my mind on the conceptual track. I imagine my reading like slot car racing. Those toy cars have small pins extending from the bottom which fit into a slot in the track. The little pin is what keeps the car on course. However, this pin can slip out of the slot, and if that happens, the car will suddenly go flying off the track. Of course this happens whenever you go too fast around a sharp corner. The trick to slot car racing then is to go as fast as you can while keeping that little pin in the slot.

Reading is like this. Speeding along through simple and familiar reading material is like racing down a straightaway. But coming into more difficult material or complex writing style means you've got to slow down, otherwise you'll find you are reading along, when all of a sudden nothing more is entering your mind. This is because you lost comprehension and slid off the track. This requires you to stop and go back to where you lost comprehension. Plus, each time you restart, you will then need to avoid the temptation to immediately lurch back to full speed; which would only cause you to lose traction, spin your wheels, and get nowhere.

Just like in racing slot cars, pushing your speed in reading can be counterproductive. The only way to read faster is to concentrate on technique by doing the following:

- Maintain concentration (pin firmly in the slot).
- Vary your speed depending on reading material (track conditions).
- Avoid mind wandering (flying off the track).
- Avoid regression (needing to put the car back).
- Gain speed gradually while you develop context (get traction).

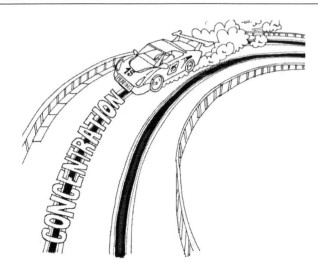

So, are there any techniques to help you get the most speed at all times, in all types of reading? Are there any specific tactics—as opposed to general strategies—some kind of reading tricks that will keep you focused and concentrated on what you are reading?

Yes, there are some techniques which can be of assistance when trying to read and comprehend faster. I mention them here not as stand-alone gimmicks for faster reading, but as things to try in context with reading phrases and concentrating on whole ideas. The most important thing is still to be totally focused on conceptualizing ideas, but these techniques can be helpful in maintaining that focus.

The Only Finger Pacer

Although most of the wacky finger waving methods so popular in many speed reading courses are laughable, it can be helpful to run your finger down the right-hand side of each page or column of text as you read. Doing this appears to be a helpful reminder as to which line your eyes should line up on next, and it also keeps you moving ahead. Try it, and see if it works for you. This does not mean forcing yourself to try to keep up with your hand—the hand *is* quicker than the brain—but use it as a gentle guide and prompt to keep your place and keep you moving forward. I personally find this one of the most helpful tricks for starting off and getting *into* the material.

And although, as I'll explain in the next chapter, the famous Evelyn Wood never recommended any of the odd-ball finger waving patterns so common in many of today's speed reading courses, she did apparently advocate this simple finger pacer technique, as evidenced in a rare occurrence she made on the What's My Line television game show on June 29th, 1961. You can watch a short, but amazing video clip of this at bit.ly/1PvoACP.

Skipping Line Ends

As your eyes approach the end of each line of text, try jumping back to the start of the next line just before your focus actually gets all the way to the last letter of the line. This doesn't mean not to read the whole line, but to trust your peripheral vision to pick it all up so that you can be processing the very end of the line during the time your eyes are moving down and across to the next line

When reading whole phrases at a time, your focus point is usually aimed somewhere near the middle of each word-group, but there can still be the tendency to continue moving your eyes to the very end of each line even after you have "read" the last phrase. This can be tricky, as you can't afford to distract yourself by mentally thinking about doing this, but you just have to be willing to let your eyes move back a bit sooner than normal.

Focusing Ahead

Focus your attention slightly ahead of each phrase. As you are processing one phrase, already be moving your focus to the next. Of course you can't go forward until you understand the previous phrase, but you can start to move your eyes slightly sooner if you think you've got it. This will tend to happen automatically when you get in the zone; your reading will begin to flow more smoothly because you will already be anticipating the next phrase.

Slowing at the Start

Start off reading slowly, being sure to imagine what you are reading in order to establish mental traction while you pick up the thread of the subject matter. Do this by spending a few nanoseconds longer on the first phrase of each sentence than those that follow. This may be too small a time period to be even consciously aware of, but you must make sure you conceptually understand what the first phrase means in order to have a better connection to where the sentence is going. This "slowing down" may ironically result in faster reading overall due to the stronger conceptual connection.

Speeding at the End

Likewise, at the end of each sentence, spend a few nanoseconds less reading it than you did the phrases before it. If you are reading in an anticipatory mode, you will likely already have predicted what the last phrase will be anyway. All you need to do is verify your suspicion and move on. You can spend that extra time picking up the thread of the next sentence. One way to do this is to mentally focus on locating the first words of sentences as you read. This will have the effect of jumping you ahead and putting a few extra nanoseconds onto these initial words.

Most of these speed adjustments are actually too tiny to consciously measure though. What you are really doing is concentrating on imagining the meaning of what you are reading and giving yourself *permission* to slow down or speed up as needed. In the end, you are primarily trying to avoid the staccato, mechanical, fixed rate of reading.

Reading Distance

Hold the reading material at a comfortable distance—close enough to be clear but also far enough to reduce unnecessary eye movement between phrases. You'll see what distance works best. This seems simple, but you will be surprised how effective proper distance is.

Stop When Necessary

Be careful not to stumble over unknown words, phrases, or ideas because these can derail your attention. Your mind will instantly respond to these mental potholes by blanking out, and nothing else will register in the text that follows.

This is one of the major sources of mental blank-out and one of the main things to look out for. Many times when you find yourself reading empty words, you will discover that if you look back a bit, you will see something in the text which was not clear to you. If you don't understand something, stop and figure it out before going on.

Relaxing

Relaxing is not actually a "trick" but is still a very important ingredient. Relaxing relates back to not allowing yourself to start pushing your speed. As much as you might want to read fast, this pressure will only serve to sabotage your efforts. It will be like trying to pull your fingers apart in those Chinese finger traps. Relax and let your speed occur as a natural result of clearer understanding for a more comfortable and enjoyable type of fast reading.

All you want to do is get the information. All reading and all writing are different. All readers are different, too. Even each time you read the same text can be different depending on many internal and external factors. In fact, because of these factors, you can never really read the "same" book twice.

Practice Exercise #17

In this exercise, let your speed vary as necessary to maintain maximum comprehension. This natural variation in speed is like an automatic transmission, where a higher or lower rpm is selected depending on changing driving conditions. Similarly, be flexible with your reading and let the content automatically choose the speed. This can mean slowing, speeding, or stopping. It can even mean going back to pick up the trail if necessary.

Also, try some of the techniques discussed in this chapter and see how they work for you. But remember, these techniques are just suggestions. If you find they work for you, great, but your primary focus should remain pursuing the ideas and letting the speed come to you.

When you're ready, begin reading the first thousand words of

Frankenstein by Mary Shelley

Frankenstein

Letter 1

To Mrs. Saville, England

St. Petersburgh, Dec. 11th, 17—

You will rejoice to hear that no disaster has accompanied the commencement of an enterprise which you have regarded with such evil forebodings. I arrived here yesterday, and my first task is to assure my dear sister of my welfare and increasing confidence in the success of my undertaking.

I am already far north of London, and as I walk in the streets of Petersburgh, I feel a cold northern breeze play upon my cheeks, which braces my nerves and fills me with delight. Do you understand this feeling? This breeze, which has traveled from the regions towards which I am advancing, gives me a foretaste of those icy climes. Inspirited by this wind of promise, my daydreams become more fervent and vivid. I try in vain to be persuaded that the pole is the seat of frost and desolation; it ever presents itself to my imagination as the region of beauty and delight. There, Margaret, the sun is forever visible, its broad disk just skirting the horizon and diffusing a perpetual splendor. There—for with your leave, my sister, I will put some trust in preceding navigators—there snow and frost are banished; and, sailing over a calm sea, we may be wafted to a land surpassing in wonders and in beauty every region hitherto discovered on the habitable globe. Its productions and features may be without example, as the phenomena of the heavenly bodies undoubtedly are in those undiscovered solitudes. What may not be expected in a country of eternal light? I may there discover the wondrous power which attracts the needle and may regulate a thousand celestial observations that require only this voyage to render their seeming eccentricities consistent forever. I shall satiate my ardent curiosity with the sight of a part of the world never before visited, and may tread a land never before imprinted by the foot of man. These are my enticements, and they are sufficient to conquer all fear of danger or death and to induce me to commence this laborious voyage with the joy a child feels when he embarks in a little boat, with his holiday mates, on an expedition of discovery up his native river. But supposing all these conjectures to be false, you cannot contest the inestimable benefit which I shall confer on all mankind, to the last generation, by discovering a passage near the pole to those countries, to reach at present so many months are requisite; or by ascertaining the secret of the magnet, which, if at all possible, can only be effected by an undertaking such as mine.

These reflections have dispelled the agitation with which I began my letter, and I feel my heart glow with an enthusiasm which elevates me to heaven, for nothing contributes so much to tranquillize the mind as a steady purpose—a point on which the soul may fix its intellectual eye. This expedition has been the favorite dream of my early years. I have read with ardor the accounts of the various voyages which have been made in the prospect of arriving at the North Pacific Ocean through the seas which surround the pole. You may remember that a history of all the voyages made for purposes of discovery composed the whole of our good Uncle Thomas' library. My education was neglected, yet I was passionately fond of reading. These volumes were my study day and night, and my familiarity with them increased that regret which I had felt, as a child, on learning that my father's dying injunction had forbidden my uncle to allow me to embark in a seafaring life.

These visions faded when I perused, for the first time, those poets whose effusions entranced my soul and lifted it to heaven. I also became a poet and for one year lived in a paradise of my own creation; I imagined that I also might obtain a niche in the temple where the names of Homer and Shakespeare are consecrated. You are well acquainted with my failure and how heavily I bore the disappointment. But just at that time I inherited the fortune of my cousin, and my thoughts were turned into the channel of their earlier bent.

Six years have passed since I resolved on my present undertaking. I can, even now, remember the hour from which I dedicated myself to this great enterprise. I commenced by inuring my body to hardship. I accompanied the whale-fishers on several expeditions to the North Sea; I voluntarily endured cold, famine, thirst, and want of sleep; I often worked harder than the common sailors during the day and devoted my nights to the study of mathematics, the theory of medicine, and those branches of physical science from which a naval adventurer might derive the greatest practical advantage. Twice I actually hired myself as an under-mate hired myself as an under-mate in a Greenland whaler, and acquitted myself to admiration. I must own I felt a little proud when my captain offered me the second dignity in the vessel and entreated me to remain with the greatest earnestness, so valuable did he consider my services. And now, dear Margaret, do I not deserve to accomplish some great purpose? My life might have been passed in ease and luxury, but I preferred glory to every enticement that wealth placed in my path. Oh, that some encouraging voice would answer in the affirmative! My courage and my resolution is firm; but my hopes fluctuate, and my spirits are often depressed. I am about to proceed on a long and difficult voyage, the emergencies of which will demand all my fortitude: I am required not only to raise the spirits of others, but sometimes to sustain...

Chapter 18: Mythical Exercises

The field of speed reading, and by extension much of the whole arena of reading improvement, has been somewhat tarnished by several misconceptions and misrepresentations. I would prefer not to be critical, but without addressing these myths, I am concerned that the information in this book—since it departs from many of these "accepted" practices—may result in questions, confusions, or misunderstandings.

Here are some of the most persistent myths which should be debunked in order to begin making real progress in your reading improvement.

Push Your Speed

Pushing your speed is the main thrust of most speed reading courses. It's presented as a habit to develop. Some suggest that once you develop the habit of seeing words faster, your comprehension will adapt to this higher speed and improve on its own.

You are told that you can reach any reading speed you wish this way, particularly if you increase in small increments at a time. Some examples suggest that a mechanical metronome is all that is needed to teach yourself to read faster. Simply find your "possible" reading speed, increase the metronome by one beat per minute at each reading, and voila! You're reading faster.

After all, it's just one beat per minute; how hard could it be, right? Well then, by this logic, you could use a metronome to learn to do *anything* faster. At just one more beat at a time, a runner could go from jogging along at a leisurely pace to breaking the land-speed record at the Bonneville Salt Flats.

The truth is, whenever you push your speed—no matter how incrementally you do it—you won't even be "reading," but merely waving your eyes back and forth. Pushing your speed beyond your comprehension leads to nothing more than exhaustion and frustration.

Finger Waving Patterns

This myth is a classic. It comes from the story of Evelyn Wood, who supposedly threw her book on the ground in frustration at her inability to learn to read as fast as the incredible speeds of a professor she knew. Then, as the story goes, after collecting her composure and picking up the book, she brushed off the dirt that had gathered on the open page and suddenly had an epiphany and the secret of speed reading was born! They say that by waving her hand across the page, Evelyn suddenly began to read at "supersonic speeds."

However, none of this is true. According to a friend of hers whom I spoke with, Mrs. Wood herself said it was "baloney," made up by the folks she sold her company to. As further proof, this incredible story doesn't even appear in Evelyn's own 1958 book, *Reading Skills*, in which she mentions nothing about any of the now classic finger waving patterns.

However, if you look in *The Evelyn Wood Seven-Day Speed Reading and Learning Program*, written in 1990 by Stanley D. Frank, ED.D, you will find plenty of descriptions of "The Famous—and fundamental—Evelyn Wood speed-reading hand motions, with illustrative diagrams." In chapter five, you not only learn the "Underlining Hand Motion," but then move on to the "'S' Hand Motion," the "Question Mark," the "'X' Hand Motion," the "Loop Hand Motion," the "'L' Hand Motion," as well as a brief discussion of the "Horseshoe," the "'U' Hand Motion," the "Brush," and the "Half-Moon."

Of course, Wood's original hand-waving pattern was supposedly the Brush (brushing off the book). If you have trouble making this one work, perhaps you need to try it with the book she was reading at the time— *Green Mansions*. Maybe it only worked with that book. Or maybe you only need to try some of the other patterns, like the "Zigzag," the "Vertical Wave," the "Double Margin," or the "Lazy S."

The reason Evelyn Wood never mentioned any of these patterns in her own book is because she never recommended them as a way to read faster. Unfortunately, as a paid spokesperson for the new owners of her Reading Dynamics company, she never publicly disclaimed them, either, and so they entered speed reading lore as a sort of speed reading creation myth.

Eye Exercises

Following Javal's discovery in 1879—that faster readers made fewer saccades as their eyes moved across each line of text—instructors began striving to train everyone to change their eye movements. Students were told over and over that they must "widen the eye span" and were put through a wide variety of exercises to do so. They would intensely strain to widen their fields of vision, forcing their eyes to almost bulge out of their sockets. But the only result of these exercises (besides possibly a severe headache) was that they could barely concentrate on what they were reading.

The same was true of the many exercises meant to train the eyes to move faster. The eyes have always been quicker than the mind. Regardless of how wide your eye span is, or how fast you move your eyes, there is nothing to see until your mind sees it.

The fallacy of trying to change the physical movement of the eyes is a classic case of treating the symptom rather than the cause. Eye movements in reading are simply the symptoms of the mental processes the person uses while reading. The eyes are only servants of the mind. Concentrate on seeing whole ideas, and the eyes will comply by automatically fixing on the appropriate sets of words.

Don't concentrate on the symptom; focus on the mental process of seeing ideas and let your eyes do their job on their own.

Subvocalization Distractions

Verbalizing or subvocalizing is often considered the bane of reading improvement. How wonderful if we could eliminate this one most destructive habit! And how easy it is to do according to several speed reading courses—just distract yourself. Believe it or not, it is common to suggest that if you were to repeat nonsense sounds aloud while you read, then you would not be able to internally hear the sounds of the words you were reading.

For example, one course recommends reciting the vowels while you read a book; say, "A E I O U" over and over while you follow your finger across each line of text. I couldn't even understand what I was reading if someone else were standing in the room reciting vowels, let alone if I were doing it myself. Where is the common sense?

If you want to read faster, you need all the concentration you can muster. You aren't going to help things if you are distracting yourself with verbal gibberish.

Skipping Unimportant Words

One suggestion to read faster is to simply read *fewer words*; this is accomplished by skipping all those "unimportant" words. But if you are going to skip any words at all, you first have to know *which* words you are going to skip. That means you have to check each word to see if it's unimportant. This seems to defeat the purpose, since you have to at least peek at each word to see if you can ignore it.

Not only is this method unworkable, but even attempting to concentrate on this word filtering process would subtract a lot of mental energy that could be used for comprehension. Plus, there is a good chance that you might skip some words that were actually very important to the text's meaning—words that could completely alter the essence of what you read.

And besides, if it were really possible to speak or write with fewer words, I'm sure we would be speaking and writing that way already—why would we continue to waste our time with all those worthless and avoidable, unimportant words?

PhotoReading

PhotoReading was developed by Paul Scheele in 1993 and claims to teach you how to read with only a quick glance at each page. It sounds like this would be wonderful, but so would the ability to fly with only the help of a Superman cape.

Some people have shown they have the ability to read this fast. The most famous was Kim Peek, who read and remembered more than nine thousand books at a speed of about ten seconds per page, with each eye scanning its own page independently! But Kim was a savant. Savant syndrome is a rare but extraordinary condition in which persons with serious mental disabilities, including autism, have some "island of genius" which stands out from the general population. There have probably been fewer than one hundred real savants in the past century. Even though savants appear to have incredible reading skills, they are "reading without reckoning."

There is one interesting fact about savants which might have a strange bearing on reading with the right brain. A few people have actually become savants later in life, often after suffering damage to the brain's left hemisphere. It seems, perhaps, that shutting off certain left-brain activities might have somehow liberated previously latent right-brain skills. This means that those exceptional skills may lie dormant, to some degree, in all of us, so perhaps by purposefully applying our imagination and visual skills, we are activating those very areas which savants are using. (This is just a thought, but please don't give yourself a brain injury to try this.)

PhotoReading among the non-savant population, however, has never been proven. In fact, PhotoReading was specifically studied by the NASA Ames Research Center and researchers came to the following conclusion:

"These results clearly indicate that there is no benefit to using the PhotoReading technique. The extremely rapid reading rates claimed by PhotoReaders were not observed; indeed, the reading rates were generally comparable to those for normal reading. Moreover, the PhotoReading experts showed an *increase* in reading time with the PhotoReading technique in comparison to normal reading. This increase in reading time was accompanied by a decrease in text comprehension. These results were found for two standardized tests of text comprehension and for three matched sets of expository texts."

In the end, as a course of study for improving your reading, I would suggest that pursuing better comprehension is going to lead to a lot more success than trying to become a savant.

Practice Exercise #18

I really wish there *were* some secret magical ways to *instantly* read faster and avoid the necessity of exercise and practice, but gimmicks only waste the little precious time we have available for making real improvement. Instead, exercise your comprehension skills by concentrating on meaning in order to improve your real reading speed.

Practice with this next exercise and continue to focus your attention on imagining the meaning of each phrase. Faster reading comes from broadening that information channel, widening it from the narrow word-by-word method to passing along whole concepts and ideas at a time.

Note: The following exercise, although taken from a fascinating and popular novel, <u>may not be suitable for children</u> due to the nature of the subject matter. It was included here because it is a compelling piece of literature that does a good job of keeping the reader's attention.

When you're ready, begin reading the first thousand words of

The Scarlet Pimpernel by Baroness Orczy

The Scarlet Pimpernel

PARIS: SEPTEMBER, 1792

A surging, seething, murmuring crowd of beings that are human only in name, for to the eye and ear they seem naught but savage creatures, animated by vile passions and by the lust of vengeance and of hate. The hour, some little time before sunset, and the place, the West Barricade, at the very spot where, a decade later, a proud tyrant raised an undying monument to the nation's glory and his own vanity.

During the greater part of the day guillotine had been kept busy at its ghastly work: all that France had boasted of in the past centuries, of ancient names, and blue blood, had paid toll to her desire for liberty and for fraternity. The carnage had only ceased at this late hour of the day because there were other more interesting sights for the people to witness, a little while before the final closing of the barricades for the night.

And so the crowd rushed away from the Place de la Greve and made for the various barricades in order to watch this interesting and amusing sight.

It was to be seen every day, for those aristos were such fools! They were traitors to the people of course, all of them, men, women, and children, who happened to be descendants of the great men who since the Crusades had made the glory of France: her old **NOBLESSE**. Their ancestors had oppressed the people, had crushed them under the scarlet heels of their dainty buckled shoes, and now the people had become the rulers of France and crushed their former masters—not beneath their heel, for they went shoeless mostly in these days—but a more effectual weight, the knife of the guillotine.

And daily, hourly, the hideous instrument of torture claimed its many victims—old men, young women, tiny children until the day when it would finally demand the head of a King and of a beautiful young Queen.

But this was as it should be: were not the people now the rulers of France? Every aristocrat was a traitor, as his ancestors had been before him: for two hundred years now the people had sweated, and toiled, and starved, to keep a lustful court in lavish extravagance; now the descendants of those who had helped to make those courts brilliant had to hide for their lives—to fly, if they wished to avoid the tardy vengeance of the people.

And they did try to hide, and tried to fly: that was just the fun of the whole thing. Every afternoon before the gates closed and the market carts went out in procession by the various barricades, some fool of an aristo endeavored to evade the clutches of the Committee of Public Safety. In various disguises, under various pretexts, they tried to slip through the barriers, which were so well guarded by citizen soldiers of the Republic. Men in women's clothes, women in male attire, children disguised in beggars' rags: there were some of all sorts: CI-DEVANT counts, marquises, even dukes, who wanted to fly from France, reach England or some other equally accursed country, and there try to rouse foreign feelings against the glorious Revolution, or to raise an army in order to liberate the wretched prisoners in the Temple, who had once called themselves sovereigns of France.

But they were nearly always caught at the barricades, Sergeant Bibot especially at the West Gate had a wonderful nose for scenting an aristo in the most perfect disguise. Then, of course, the fun began. Bibot would look at his prey as a cat looks upon the mouse, play with him, sometimes for quite a quarter of an hour, pretend to be hoodwinked by the disguise, by the wigs and other bits of theatrical make-up which hid the identity of a CI-DEVANT noble marquise or count.

Oh! Bibot had a keen sense of humor, and it was well worth hanging round that West Barricade, in order to see him catch an aristo in the very act of trying to flee from the vengeance of the people.

Sometimes Bibot would let his prey actually out by the gates, allowing him to think for the space of two minutes at least that he really had escaped out of Paris, and might even manage to reach the coast of England in safety, but Bibot would let the unfortunate wretch walk about ten meters towards the open country, then he would send two men after him and bring him back, stripped of his disguise.

Oh! That was extremely funny, for as often as not the fugitive would prove to be a woman, some proud marchioness, who looked terribly comical when she found herself in Bibot's clutches after all, and knew that a summary trial would await her the next day and after that, the fond embrace of Madame la Guillotine.

No wonder that on this fine afternoon in September the crowd round Bibot's gate was eager and excited. The lust of blood grows with its satisfaction, there is no satiety: the crowd had seen a hundred noble heads fall beneath the guillotine today, it wanted to make sure that it would see another hundred fall on the morrow.

Bibot was sitting on an overturned and empty cask close by the gate of the barricade; a small detachment of citizen soldiers was under his command. The work had been very hot lately. Those cursed aristos were becoming terrified and tried their hardest to slip out of Paris: men, women and children, whose ancestors, even in remote ages, had served those traitorous Bourbons, were all traitors themselves and right food for the guillotine. Every day Bibot had had the satisfaction of unmasking some fugitive royalists and sending them back to be tried by the Committee of Public Safety, presided over by that good patriot, Citoyen Foucquier-Tinville.

Robespierre and Danton...

Chapter 19: Mythical Stories

There are so many amazing stories about speed reading, in fact about reading in general. That is one reason this book includes a discussion about what reading is and how it works, to help to demonstrate why these stories are so preposterous.

Reading is a more complex mental task then many people realize. It's actually pretty amazing that it's possible at all.

At the same time, reading faster is also a lot simpler than is often expected. It's not learned by a bunch of bizarre exercises, but by simply learning to focus your attention on the meaning of what you read.

Let's go over some of the popular speed reading stories and see why they don't make sense.

Thousands of Words per Minute

It's unfortunate that the business of helping people improve their reading skills has been hijacked by so many charlatans. The myth that we can learn to read at freakishly fast speeds is continually perpetrated in order to sell the maximum number of books and courses.

For example, here is a sample claim from one speed reading book: *"Read at any speed you wish to from 1 to 20,000 words per minute, dependent entirely upon your reading goals."*

"Entirely upon your *goals*"? Well then you wouldn't need the book, would you? All you need is the goal! Choose the goal and you're done. And then, what about that low range of ONE word per minute? That actually sounds more difficult than the twenty thousand (and I also suppose twenty thousand and *one* would be completely out of the question).

As proof of how successful their methods are, the same book lists the "World's Top Ten Speed Readers." Their listed speeds range between

1,560 and 3,850 words per minute (not 20,000 though). However, none of these names show up on a Google search, making it sound like these top ten amazing readers were only known to the author of that book.

It is not necessary to name this book because these claims are not unusual, and you would have no problem confirming this with your own research.

The biggest problem with claims like these is that they become the common expectation of people when they think of speed reading. These types of results are not true, and they end up costing people in lost time and money and in their unfortunate feelings of frustration.

When people learn that it's not possible to read thousands of words per minute, they figure, "Why bother trying to improve at all?"

Well, think of it like this. Imagine you have a painful limp and any walking is a frustrating and difficult chore. In fact, everywhere you go, you have to resort to using crutches just to keep from falling down.

Then, a therapist tells you she can help. She can show you some exercises that will cure you. With these exercises, you will be able to walk with ease, go wherever you want, explore all the places that were out of reach before—and even run if you wish—without pain. You could throw those crutches away.

It would be a dream come true, but you would turn her down. You would say, "Walking is not fast enough. I want to run at super-human speeds like the Flash in the DC comic books! I want to run so fast that my friends will be amazed. And besides, I've heard that I could learn to do this in sixty minutes with just a few secret running tricks."

So you hobble out of the therapist's office, taking your crutches with you.

Well, where are all these Flashes? Where are all these people whose only reading limit is how fast they can flip pages?

Give up your belief in comics. Instead, throw away the crutches of subvocalizing and regression, and begin to enjoy your reading. Explore all the information out there waiting to be discovered without the pain of exhaustion and frustration.

Real speed reading is six hundred to one thousand words per minute, and most people find four hundred words per minute a stubborn hurtle.

But why continue stumbling along at less than two hundred words per minute, and with poor comprehension, if there is a way to make reading a joy rather than a chore?

And who knows? Maybe you can be one of those who reach the thousand words per minute mark. If so, you still have to pass four hundred first. To do that, you need to put on the coveralls and do the work. But regardless of your ultimate achievement, any improvement in your reading speed and comprehension can have a powerful effect on many aspects of your life.

The truth may be a disappointment to some, but in the end, reality is always easier to handle than delusion.

Comprehension Follows Speed

This is actually pretty amazing when you think about it, but doesn't it seem like hardly anybody is concentrating on teaching readers to *comprehend* better? Instead, they usually suggest that your comprehension will magically improve *after* you learn to "read" faster.

Here's a passage from a popular speed reading book: *"If you have difficulty with concentration and comprehension… go faster rather than more slowly, and you may find a great improvement."*

In the same book, it instructs, *"Practice as fast as you can for 1 minute, not worrying about comprehension."*

In another book, the author says, *"Research is increasingly showing that the faster you read, the better your comprehension."*

And then another shouts, *"DO NOT CONCERN YOURSELF WITH COMPREHENSION."*

Actually, this is the overwhelming advice in speed reading books and courses.

But does this make sense to anyone? Whose research is this? Research could also show that faster racecar drivers had better skills, but which came first? Wouldn't it make more sense that skill led to speed, rather than vice versa?

Comprehension Tests

Most speed reading courses will include comprehension tests. They have you read a passage and then ask you to answer questions about the passage. But these comprehension tests are ineffective. They are not only a waste of time; they are often used to fool students into thinking they have improved their reading.

Ineffective

It would certainly be important to know whether or not you understood what you have read. How awful to spend hours reading a book and, only after finishing it, find out that you didn't understand anything. What a waste of time! But just as when I'm listening to somebody talk, when I'm reading, I generally know if I'm getting it or not—in real time, not after I take some test.

The main problem with comprehension tests is that they are really testing other things besides comprehension—things such as memory and even test-taking skills.

Comprehension tests generally consist of a list of multiple choice or true-false questions at the end of a reading assignment. The problem with such tests is that so much depends on your previous knowledge of the content. And nearly as much depends on your ability to guess which facts you should probably remember for the test.

And not all people would pay attention to the exact same things. For example, an article about 3D printers would be viewed very differently by an engineer, a salesman, and an investor. Each would pay attention to and remember, either, how it works, who would buy one, or what its business growth potential was.

However even though each of us reads for our own reasons, we all know while we are reading whether or not we are grasping the information that's important to us.

Deceptive

Not only are comprehension tests poor indicators of comprehension, but they are sometimes used to deceive students into thinking they have improved when they haven't.

The trick is to make the initial test more difficult than the final one, giving the indication that the student's comprehension has "improved."

For example, the first reading test is often loaded with names, numbers, and lists; whereas the final test can be of a more general nature, resulting in the kinds of questions you could likely answer correctly even if you didn't read the article.

Again, I'll use an example from a popular speed reading book. There are ten reading tests throughout this particular book.

The article for the first test is nineteen hundred words long and contains:

- 43 numbers
- 32 proper names
- 2 bulleted lists (twenty and seven items long)
- 11 comma-delimited lists (i.e. *"to problem solve, to analyze, to prioritize, to create and to communicate"*) with up to eleven items on each list

Not only is the article difficult, but many of the questions are misleading. For example, question one on the first test reads, *"True or false? The top eighty percent of British companies invest considerable money and time in training."*

The correct answer is "false," but take a look at the text from the article: *"... of the top 10% of British companies, 80% invested considerable money and time in training..."*

It says eighty percent of the *top ten percent!* That is a sneaky trap. And also notice that the number "80" is used in the text, but the word "eighty" is used in the question.

Additionally, the suggestion before taking that first test is, *"Don't worry about getting low scores in either speed or comprehension."* So a student would obviously show improvement on the last test because before reading the last article, students are instructed to *"Just trust yourself and read as fast as you possibly can."*

Plus, this last article is easier to read and has easier questions. The last article is only fourteen hundred words long (three-quarters the length of the first), much more general in nature, and only contains:

- 5 numbers
- 2 proper names
- No lists

And the questions are absolute softballs. This trick of unequal tests is used by many speed reading courses. They multiply your reading speed by your comprehension percent to establish your "effective" speed. By making the last test easier than the first, they make is seem as if you have made a miraculous improvement during the course!

What's worse is that this "improvement" is quite often used to disqualify you for any refund, the wording of which typically sounds something like, "Double your *effective* reading speed or your money back."

JFK the Speed Reader

It's amazing that this popular speed reading myth has gone on so long. Many speed reading books and courses tell the story of how President Kennedy took the Evelyn Wood course and learned to read twelve hundred words per minute. This success story has been used as proof that "You can do it, too!"

The story of JFK's reading prowess fit with the popular narrative of the time—that our new president was young, handsome, and clever—so the reading story spread quickly. The bandwagon didn't even have to slow down for dozens of other speed reading courses to hop on and quote this "fact."

But President Kennedy never read twelve hundred words per minute. This figure was only an off-the-cuff answer he gave when a reporter questioned him about his reading speed.

It's true he took the Evelyn Wood course, but he never finished it, and so he never tested his final speed. It's doubtful JFK was being intentionally dishonest; this may have been the speed at which he could skim to get the gist of material. But according to *The Causes of High and Low Reading Achievement* by Ronald P. Carver, JFK's reading speed was probably five to six hundred words per minute, an excellent reading speed but not one that belongs in the annals of speed reading legends.

The Phonics Method Causes Subvocalizing

There has long been controversy over how best to teach reading to young children. There is particular contention between the whole-word people and the phonics people. One of the aspersions cast upon the phonics folks is that by teaching kids to sound out words, they are condemning them to a life of vocalizing while they read.

One problem with that logic is that it's never been shown that whole-word students read *without* vocalizing. And you could also wonder that if the habits of adults are cast in stone as children, then why aren't we saying each letter too? Because after all, they taught us the alphabet before they taught us phonics.

Besides all that logic stuff, it just so happens that vocalizing *helps* comprehension—plain and simple. You do it every time you try to decipher anything complicated. It's natural to vocalize to make things easier to understand.

Although subvocalizing does supply a comprehension benefit, it is still a very strong habit. However, it's definitely easier to replace this habit than suppress it, and you replace it by applying your visual and imagining skills. Subvocalizing is a crutch, and you will stop using it when it is no longer needed.

Reading vs. Skimming and Scanning

If you want to learn how to *read* faster, you won't do it by practicing the piano or learning to dance. Skimming and scanning are excellent and very helpful skills to have, but they are *not* reading.

Too many "speed reading" courses intentionally confuse these skills with reading. When you push your speed and ignore your comprehension, you are skimming—not reading. When you search the text for a pertinent piece of information, you are scanning—not reading.

Yes, learn to do these things, but don't walk away thinking you were speed reading.

Practice Exercise #19

Continue to practice real speed reading through *speed comprehension.* Forget all the speed reading fables, and create your own true reading success story by involving and strengthening that powerful and often ignored silent partner on your right side.

When you're ready, begin reading the first thousand words of

Little Women by Louisa May Alcott

Little Women

"Christmas won't be Christmas without any presents," grumbled Jo, lying on the rug.

"It's so dreadful to be poor!" sighed Meg, looking down at her old dress.

"I don't think it's fair for some girls to have plenty of pretty things, and other girls nothing at all," added little Amy, with an injured sniff.

"We've got Father and Mother, and each other," said Beth contentedly from her corner.

The four young faces on which the firelight shone brightened at the cheerful words, but darkened again as Jo said sadly, "We haven't got Father, and shall not have him for a long time." She didn't say "perhaps never," but each silently added it, thinking of Father far away, where the fighting was.

Nobody spoke for a minute; then Meg said in an altered tone, "You know the reason Mother proposed not having any presents this Christmas was because it is going to be a hard winter for everyone; and she thinks we ought not to spend money for pleasure, when our men are suffering so in the army. We can't do much, but we can make our little sacrifices, and ought to do it gladly. But I am afraid I don't," and Meg shook her head, as she thought regretfully of all the pretty things she wanted.

"But I don't think the little we should spend would do any good. We've each got a dollar, and the army wouldn't be much helped by our giving that. I agree not to expect anything from Mother or you, but I do want to buy Undine and Sintran for myself. I've wanted it so long," said Jo, who was a bookworm.

"I planned to spend mine in new music," said Beth, with a little sigh, which no one heard but the hearth brush and kettle-holder.

"I shall get a nice box of Faber's drawing pencils; I really need them," said Amy decidedly.

"Mother didn't say anything about our money, and she won't wish us to give up everything. Let's each buy what we want, and have a little fun; I'm sure we work hard enough to earn it," cried Jo, examining the heels of her shoes in a gentlemanly manner.

"I know I do—teaching those tiresome children nearly all day, when I'm longing to enjoy myself at home," began Meg, in the complaining tone again.

"You don't have half such a hard time as I do," said Jo. "How would you like to be shut up for hours with a nervous, fussy old lady, who keeps you trotting, is never satisfied, and worries you till you're ready to fly out the window or cry?"

"It's naughty to fret, but I do think washing dishes and keeping things tidy is the worst work in the world. It makes me cross, and my hands get so stiff, I can't practice well at all." And Beth looked at her rough hands with a sigh that anyone could hear that time.

"I don't believe any of you suffer as I do," cried Amy, "for you don't have to go to school with impertinent girls, who plague you if you don't know your lessons, and laugh at your dresses, and label your father if he isn't rich, and insult you when your nose isn't nice."

"If you mean libel, I'd say so, and not talk about labels, as if Papa was a pickle bottle," advised Jo, laughing.

"I know what I mean, and you needn't be statirical about it. It's proper to use good words, and improve your vocabilary," returned Amy, with dignity.

"Don't peck at one another, children. Don't you wish we had the money Papa lost when we were little, Jo? Dear me! How happy and good we'd be, if we had no worries!" said Meg, who could remember better times.

"You said the other day you thought we were a deal happier than the King children, for they were fighting and fretting all the time, in spite of their money."

"So I did, Beth. Well, I think we are. For though we do have to work, we make fun of ourselves, and are a pretty jolly set, as Jo would say."

"Jo does use such slang words!" observed Amy, with a reproving look at the long figure stretched on the rug.

Jo immediately sat up, put her hands in her pockets, and began to whistle.

"Don't, Jo. It's so boyish!"

"That's why I do it."

"I detest rude, unladylike girls!"

"I hate affected, niminy-piminy chits!"

"Birds in their little nests agree," sang Beth, the peacemaker, with such a funny face that both sharp voices softened to a laugh, and the "pecking" ended for that time.

"Really, girls, you are both to be blamed," said Meg, beginning to lecture in her elder-sisterly fashion. "You are old enough to leave off boyish tricks, and to behave better, Josephine. It didn't matter so much when you were a little girl, but now you are so tall, and turn up your hair, you should remember that you are a young lady."

"I'm not! And if turning up my hair makes me one, I'll wear it in two tails till I'm twenty," cried Jo, pulling off her net, and shaking down a chestnut mane. "I hate to think I've got to grow up, and be Miss March, and wear long gowns, and look as prim as a China Aster! It's bad enough to be a girl, anyway, when I like boy's games and work and manners! I can't get over my disappointment in not being a boy. And it's worse than ever now, for I'm dying to go and fight with Papa. And I can only stay home and knit, like a poky old woman!"

And Jo shook the blue army sock till the needles rattled like castanets, and her ball bounded across the room.

"Poor Jo! It's too bad, but it can't be helped. So you must try to be contented with making your name boyish, and playing brother to us girls," said Beth, stroking the rough head with a hand that all the dish washing and dusting in the world could not make ungentle in its touch.

"As for you, Amy," continued Meg, "you are altogether too particular and prim. Your airs are funny now, but you'll grow...

Chapter 20: Reading on Your Own

The phrase-highlighted practice text in this book gives you an excellent opportunity to experience reading whole phrases and to practice visualizing and conceptualizing the ideas while you read. The final goal, however, is to be able to use this skill to read regular text, without assistance. So, what happens when you remove the training wheels and read on your own?

Practice with Normal Text

Practice reading with normal text whenever you can. This will help you transfer the skill to your regular reading. Scanning normal text for phrases will help you learn what works best for you.

Plus, you want to discover what special challenges are faced when you are in charge of both steps; not only conceptualizing whole word-groups at a glance, but simultaneously picking out those word-groups on your own.

The most common question about picking out word-groups is, "How do you know which words to put together?" And the second most popular question is, "How can you select the word-groups fast enough while also concentrating on your reading?" The answer to both is the same, and is similar to the answer on how to stop subvocalization and regression: by visualizing!

Remember that you can only concentrate on one thing at a time, and while you're reading, that one thing should only be: comprehending the text. Just as you use visualizing for replacing, rather than suppressing, bad habits, you can use visualizing for *finding* the phrases.

It may seem impossible at first, but when you look for meaningful ideas that you can visualize, your mind will automatically zoom in on the phrases for you.

Here's an example. As you read the following sentence, don't worry about your speed, but concentrate on looking for images and ideas.

Mr. Jones, of the Manor Farm, had locked the hen-houses for the night, but was too drunk to remember to shut the popholes.

Read it over if you need to in order to come up with something to imagine for each separately meaningful piece of the sentence. You're just looking at the sentence and thinking, "What could I imagine here?"

Different readers may group the words together differently, but here is one way the sentence could be read. Each line represents the words your eyes might see at a glance, but the dark text represents the part which your mind might pick out as a separate visual idea. This is an idea you could instantly imagine and conceptualize. Read each dark phrase and look at the suggested image.

Mr. Jones, of

Jones, of the Manor Farm, had

Farm, had locked the hen-house for

hen-houses for the night, but

night, but was too drunk to

drunk to remember to

remember to shut the popholes.

As shown here, there isn't really a rigid fixation on each phrase, but a general focus on larger portions of the sentence. You will be aware of the surrounding text but the units of meaning will stand out as imaginable ideas when you are looking for ideas to visualize.

The generic images above are only samples of what you might imagine; any attention paid to imagining the meaning will work, though. And remember again, not every idea has an easy to imagine picture; paying attention to just the conceptual ideas will also work.

The word-groups chosen in this example are also subjective. There is no perfect grouping, although this particular grouping may possibly be close to what many people would come up with, depending on the number of words at a time they are comfortable with. But which words you group and which images or ideas you imagine are much less important than the effort to *see* the groups of words as ideas. Just scan the text and look for ideas.

If you concentrate on seeing ideas, the words will clump together in the only way they make sense. It's a little bit like looking for all the blue sky pieces when you are making a jigsaw puzzle; you are more likely to see something if it's in the forefront of your mind and you are looking for it.

Just look for each meaningful chunk of information and you will feel your right-brain say, "Aha," as it recognizes the meaning of the phrase.

Cautions

One thing you must look out for while reading normal text is excessive speeding. Reading without the assistance of highlighted phrases is going to be slower as you obviously have more to do now. But at the same time, there will probably be an overwhelming urge to push your speed as fast as you can go. Instead, slow down and pay attention to each phrase. You must make comprehension your main, no, your *only* pursuit. Chasing after speed is chasing your shadow. Slow down if necessary, because if you aren't comprehending, you aren't reading! Make sure you are looking at the ideas and concentrating on their images and meaning; this is when the speed will come.

Another temptation—probably made even stronger when reading regular text—is to take in too many words at once. It will seem to be an easy way to read faster, by simply reading larger phrases, but you need to let the visualizing right brain decide where the ideas are, even if you end up only picking one or two words at times. Yes, I said even one word, because the goal is to visualize ideas as you read, and multi-word phrases are used only because they are easier to visualize. But sometimes even a single word can represent a separate distinct thought. Just be flexible and patient and look for the conceptual ideas while you read.

Lastly, you may find it difficult to enforce phrase-reading, and instead may try to *flow* through the text in a steady stream of individual words. It's true that the more you concentrate on ideas of whole word-groups, the more you will get into the "zone"—where the *ideas* will become a smooth flow—but in order to do that, you must be looking at the text in distinct phrases. Be sure to focus your attention on those meaningful phrases that you can imagine as visual, conceptual ideas. Even if this is strangely difficult to adhere to, you must correct yourself if you notice that you are running individual words together in a steady string. Isolating the distinct phrases is just as important to comprehension speed as is having spaces between words. Don't ignore the phrases—they are like the cogs in the comprehension gears.

Types of Reading

So what kinds of reading can you apply this to? Well, it's probably not for reading small items like street signs or product ingredients. But the more continuous the flow of ideas, the more reading for ideas will help you see the bigger picture. And although this can be used for many types of reading, each type may still require a somewhat different approach.

Educational

Reading educational material requires a higher degree of flexibility than most reading. The very nature of educational reading is meant to be one of discovery. All of this type of reading must be new to you in order for it to even be educational.

Any type of non-fiction reading is going to include frequent stops to ponder what you have read. This stop-and-go reading is naturally going to increase the time it takes to finish such a book, but you are doing more than just reading; you are also stopping to consider what you have read. Regardless of the overall speed, reading in phrases can make any complicated material easier to understand by breaking it up into meaningful, bite-size pieces of information.

Just remember to stop when necessary to carefully consider something you have learned. Also, make sure to start off slowly when you begin again, ensuring you are paying attention to the new material rather than the old.

Current Events

Keeping up with the news can involve a lot more skimming than reading. There is so much news available that you have to be very selective. Glance at headlines and skim articles that look interesting, reading only the few that merit deeper understanding. Even then, you should always be ready to drop it and move on.

Personal Interest

Personal interest reading could include most pastime reading, such as hobbies, sports, or entertainment. Even more than with current events, this type of reading needs a ruthless filtering because much of it you will already know—or at least suspect. This type of reading is more like a treasure hunt. Skim until you find the nuggets of novelty, and don't hesitate to put the material down if you decide it is not offering you anything new or helpful.

Stories

This is where you can lose yourself in your reading. Whether it's fiction or non-fiction, reading a story is like watching a movie. This is where it's easiest to get into the zone, a mental place where the rest of the world simply falls away. You can tune out everything and enter this new world. Here is where reading with your right brain will turn *listening* to a story into *living* it.

Your imagination and visualized ideas will make you a part of the story, and your faster reading will make the story move along more fluidly. You won't be pushing your speed; your speed will increase as you are being pulled through the story.

Comics

How could you speed read a comic book, and why would you? It's a funny thing about reading in phrases, but it becomes a habit. And when faced with a small balloon of text, it is often natural to see it as a whole idea and read it all at once. I was surprised when I first noticed this, but I suppose the word bubbles in comics are already more like phrases than long dissertations. And then, if you're not in a rush, you could use the extra time to enjoy the pictures.

Last Words

And finally, a few last words to keep in mind. Realize that reading for ideas won't always work perfectly. It is not magic. It is a tool to help you focus and concentrate on ideas rather than words. As such, it will be a much more effective way of reading than concentrating on the words and the sounds they make. Look for the ideas and they will appear; realize that a lot depends on the type of text, the type of writer, and even (maybe especially) your own frame of mind. Reading for ideas is the path to better and faster comprehension, and the more you take this path, the smoother it will become.

Two other things that can be helpful while you practice are to set small reading goals and take regular breaks. Pick up a book and decide how many pages you are going to read. Put a bookmark at that ending page and then stop when you get there—but not *until* you get there. Don't stop and don't let any other thoughts interfere with your reading until you reach that bookmark. Train yourself during these short sprints to only think of what you are reading. Do as many sprints as you want in one sitting, but allow yourself a breather between each. Make it a habit to only *read* while you read. Make the action of picking up a book an automatic switch that toggles your mind into its reader mode.

And again, remember also to be patient with yourself. It is self-defeating to criticize your performance because you are only reinforcing those negative ideas. Being impatient also increases the urge to push your speed beyond of your comprehension.

It is good to critique yourself, if that means to honestly appraise your strengths and weaknesses, but if you find yourself being overly self-critical, then stop reading and do something else until you can approach your reading practice with a more productive attitude.

Also, realize that you are not responsible for all your reading success. It is a tango between you and the author. It is an unfortunate truth, but many authors do not write as fluently as we might like. As Nathaniel Hawthorne put it, "Easy reading is damn hard writing." No matter how hard you try, some text is just slower to understand and read. And today, with so much writing and so many writers, thanks to the internet and self-publishing, I'm sure you've noticed that there are surprising amounts of poor spelling, poor grammar, and even typing errors.

But that's the way it is. Do the best with what you have. Some of these texts, littered with grammatical land mines, may still contain enough amazing gems of information to make the effort worthwhile. Just be patient and flexible.

You will succeed because success is simply being on the right path. If you know what you need to do, then you only have to do it. What you need to do is read text as ideas by visualizing whole units of meaning. That's it. The rest is practice.

I hope this book has given you some new tools as well as a new perspective on reading. All reading takes place in our brains, not our eyes. Our eyes are only tools for delivering the text to our brains, the same way our hands are tools for holding the book. Real reading only takes place when information is integrated into our existing knowledge base. This internal process of information assimilation is where all real reading improvement has to take place, not in any external changes like the speed at which we move our eyes or the width of our "eye span."

Reading IS comprehension. That means comprehension is not just a part of reading, it is all that reading is. If we read text with fifty percent comprehension, then we are only reading fifty percent of the text. The rest of the text is only looked at—and maybe sounded out—but not "read."

Once that text enters the brain, it's not inside some mysterious black box where we have no control of how it is processed. Much of what goes on in our brains may be outside our conscious view; what goes on may be mysterious, but it's *not* out of our control. We might not be able to control exactly how our brains process text, but we can steer them in more productive directions, the same way a rider directs a horse. The rider doesn't have to know what the horse is thinking, but by understanding the horse's capabilities and by using proper techniques, he can cause the horse to do his bidding. By understanding reading and understanding your brain, you can read for ideas by reading with the right brain.

Practice Exercise #20

We now arrive at our last practice exercise, but remember, there is still a lot of skill to gain by going back over the exercises and reapplying your improved reading habits.

When you're ready, begin reading the first thousand words of

Anna Karenina by Leo Tolstoy

Anna Karenina

Happy families are all alike; every unhappy family is unhappy in its own way.

Everything was in confusion in the Oblonskys' house. The wife had discovered that the husband was carrying on an intrigue with a French girl, who had been a governess in their family, and she had announced to her husband that she could not go on living in the same house with him. This position of affairs had now lasted three days, and not only the husband and wife themselves, but all the members of their family and household, were painfully conscious of it. Every person in the house felt that there was no sense in their living together, and that the stray people brought together by chance in any inn had more in common with one another than they, the members of the family and household of the Oblonskys. The wife did not leave her own room; the husband had not been at home for three days. The children ran wild all over the house; the English governess quarreled with the housekeeper, and wrote to a friend asking her to look out for a new situation for her; the man-cook had walked off the day before just at dinner time; the kitchen-maid, and the coachman had given warning.

Three days after the quarrel, Prince Stepan Arkadyevitch Oblonsky— Stiva, as he was called in the fashionable world—woke up at his usual hour, that is, at eight o'clock in the morning, not in his wife's bedroom, but on the leather-covered sofa in his study. He turned over his stout, well-cared-for person on the springy sofa, as though he would sink into a long sleep again; he vigorously embraced the pillow on the other side and buried his face in it; but all at once he jumped up, sat up on the sofa, and opened his eyes.

"Yes, yes, how was it now?" he thought, going over his dream. "Now, how was it? To be sure! Alabin was giving a dinner at Darmstadt; no, not Darmstadt, but something American. Yes, but then, Darmstadt was in America. Yes, Alabin was giving a dinner on glass tables, and the tables sang, Il mio tesoro—not Il mio tesoro though, but something better, and there were some sort of little decanters on the table, and they were women, too," he remembered.

Stepan Arkadyevitch's eyes twinkled gaily, and he pondered with a smile. "Yes, it was nice, very nice. There was a great deal more that was delightful, only there's no putting it into words, or even expressing it in one's thoughts awake." And noticing a gleam of light peeping in beside one of the serge curtains, he cheerfully dropped his feet over the edge of the sofa, and felt about with them for his slippers, a present on his last birthday, worked for him by his wife on gold-colored morocco. And, as he had done every day for the last nine years, he stretched out his hand, without getting up, towards the place where his dressing-gown always hung in his bedroom. And thereupon he suddenly remembered that he was not sleeping in his wife's room, but in his study, and why: the smile vanished from his face, he knitted his brows.

"Ah, ah, ah! Oo!..." he muttered, recalling everything that had happened. And again every detail of his quarrel with his wife was present to his imagination, all the hopelessness of his position, and worst of all, his own fault.

"Yes, she won't forgive me, and she can't forgive me. And the most awful thing about it is that it's all my fault—all my fault, though I'm not to blame. That's the point of the whole situation," he reflected. "Oh, oh, oh!" he kept repeating in despair, as he remembered the acutely painful sensations caused him by this quarrel.

Most unpleasant of all was the first minute when, on coming, happy and good-humored, from the theater, with a huge pear in his hand for his wife, he had not found his wife in the drawing-room, to his surprise had not found her in the study either, and saw her at last in her bedroom with the unlucky letter that revealed everything in her hand.

She, his Dolly, forever fussing and worrying over household details, and limited in her ideas, as he considered, was sitting perfectly still with the letter in her hand, looking at him with an expression of horror, despair, and indignation.

"What's this? This?" she asked, pointing to the letter.

And at this recollection, Stepan Arkadyevitch, as is so often the case, was not so much annoyed at the fact itself as at the way in which he had met his wife's words.

There happened to him at that instant what does happen to people when they are unexpectedly caught in something very disgraceful. He did not succeed in adapting his face to the position in which he was placed towards his wife by the discovery of his fault. Instead of being hurt, denying, defending himself, begging forgiveness, instead of remaining indifferent even—anything would have been better than what he did do—his face utterly involuntarily (reflex spinal action, reflected Stepan Arkadyevitch, who was fond of physiology)—utterly involuntarily assumed its habitual, good-humored, and therefore idiotic smile.

This idiotic smile he could not forgive himself. Catching sight of that smile, Dolly shuddered as though at physical pain, broke out with her characteristic heat into a flood of cruel words, and rushed out of the room. Since then she had refused to see her husband.

"It's that idiotic smile that's to blame for it all," thought Stepan Arkadyevitch.

"But what's to be done? What's to be done?" he said to himself in despair, and found no answer. Stepan Arkadyevitch was a truthful man in his relations with himself. He was incapable of deceiving himself and...

Additional Resources

Free Speed Reading Course

There's a free online course available to help you further develop your phrase-reading skills.

The books, "Speed Reading with the Right Brain," "Easy Speed Reading," and "Speed Reading in 60 Seconds" are convenient, real life opportunities to practice phrase-reading in actual books — however, an online course can do things that books can't.

This course includes 12 unique lessons consisting of 15 exercises each. The lessons progress step by step from a one-phrase-at-a-time display, until you are reading with a black-and-gray display as used in this book.

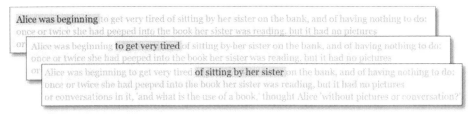

Each exercise takes on average, approximately two minutes to complete. Therefore, the entire course consists of about six hours' practice which will give you an excellent opportunity to learn to read and understand whole phrases at a time.

- Join over 75,000 users of this free online course.
- Over 500 books in the library to choose from
- Enter your own text if you prefer
- Get instant feedback of both your speed
- Even get feedback of your concentration level

This is one of the most unique reading systems you will find anywhere!

Sign up for your free course now at **readspeeder.com**.

Free Phrase-Reading Tool

There's also a free online phrase-reading tool into which you can paste any text you wish to read faster. This tool will automatically display the text one meaningful phrase at a time, and allow you to adjust the speed as you go.

Once again, this is no substitute for book practice, but you'll find that when you pick up a book after some practice with this tool, that you'll naturally be reading faster because your mind will become used to reading whole phrases at a faster speed.

This is not only an excellent practice device, but can also be used just to get through those long online articles faster.

Copy and paste any text into the tool. Then sit back and read as easily as watching a video. Speed reading has never been easier.

- Practice phrase-reading with your own text
- Use with any text you wish to read
- Speed through those long blog or news articles
- Pause, rewind, or change speeds at any time
- Sit back and watch text like it was a video

Start using this free tool now at **phrasereader.com**.

EASY SPEED READING
With 12 Fun Excerpts of Popular Fiction

Available in eBook or paperback at **amzn.to/28ZcHF0**

Build on your phrase-reading skills by practicing with some fun and easy fiction reading. Enjoy 12 excerpts from popular Fantasy, Sci-Fi, Mystery and Romance, while you firmly develop your new skill into a long-term habit.

Comprehension is *always* paramount, but these stories are intended to make it as easy as possible to practice your speed reading. Here's the chance to see how fast you can really read.

Each excerpt is exactly 2,000 words long, so that you can easily compare your speed results. This also means that when you complete any exercise in two minutes, 20 seconds; you will be reading 600 wpm, the official threshold of real "speed reading."

- See how fast you can really read.
- Enjoy fun fiction stories as a mental movie.
- Learn what it feels like to get into that special reading "zone."

236

SPEED READING IN 60 SECONDS
100 One-Minute Speed Reading Sprints

Available in eBook or paperback at **amzn.to/2c2q7CM**

No time to practice? You can do these practice exercises whenever you have one minute free. These 100 60-second drills are perfect little phrase-highlighted excerpts to test your skills.

Each excerpt is 600 words, and as such, make a simple read-speeding target to read in 60 seconds in order to be speed-reading at 600 wpm.

Take a minute practice whenever you have time to cement a life-long reading habit.

Here's How This Book Can Help You.

- Speed reading is 600 wpm.
- Each of these 100 excerpts is 600 words long.
- Read them in 60 seconds... and you're speed reading!

Discover what real speed reading feels like, when your mind adapts by paying more attention to phrases and ideas than to words and sounds.

Your Review

Book reviews are very important to a book's success, and your review would mean a lot to me.

If you have time, please go to **amazon.com/review/create-review?asin=B00O3OD5WY** and leave at least a few short words about this book.

Your book reviews not only help the author, but they can also be a convenient way for you to keep track of your books at **amazon.com/gp/cdp/member-reviews**.

I've found the habit of reviewing books I like, to be very helpful in keeping my library organized and in saving time finding those books I've enjoyed.

Thanks again for reading my book and feel free to contact me any time with any questions or comments about Speed Reading with the Right Brain at **db@readspeeder.com**

About the Author

David Butler is a retired mechanical design engineer. He has applied his conceptual approach for solving design engineering problems to developing a solution to his lifelong struggle with slow reading. He enjoys sharing this solution with others not only through this book but with the free online reading course and online reading tool.

David lives in the scenic mountain forest of Southern California, but whenever the weather is 75° and sunny, he can usually be found riding his beach bike along the ocean with his beautiful wife.

50273045R00135

Made in the USA
Middletown, DE
28 October 2017